Love Your Gay Neighbor

Instructions from the Bible

Daniel V. Runyon, Ph.D.

Love your Gay Neighbor:
Instructions from the Bible
Daniel V. Runyon, Ph.D.

Copyright 2015 by Daniel V. Runyon

The Voice™: Scripture taken from The Voice™. Copyright ©2006, 2007, 2008, 2012 by Ecclesia Bible Society.

Saltbox Press
Spring Arbor, Michigan 49283
Print price: $9.99 USD
Print ISBN: 978-1516910465

Both eBook and print versions of this and other works by this author are available online. Search Amazon.com: Daniel V. Runyon: Books.

Context

Nothing but vanity from your prophets—
nothing but worthlessness from them; They
never *warned and* exposed you to correct your
wicked ways so that *things would go well again*
with no captivity. Instead, they told divine
oracles of lies and deceit, *that everything was
fine.*

—Lamentations 2:14

Dedication

To my lifelong friend Dwight who models the kind of love explored in these pages.

Acknowledgments

Thanks to all who wisely guided my pen through this minefield: Linda Adams, Dwight Metzger, Anne Paine-Root, M. Renée Runyon, Brenda Young, and Denny. Unforeseen repercussions will be due to my own missteps.

Contents

Preface

Love Your Gay Neighbor tells the story of God, finds a reliable definition of love, shows how people in the Bible demonstrate that love, and equips you to love your gay neighbors.

You will find answers to such questions as these: "What happened to God? What caused Him to punish and destroy homosexuals in earlier times? Why does He write such things in his Book—what things happened that resulted in Him feeling the way He does about homosexual behavior?"

An equally important question is this: "If God hates sin so much, why is He so patient with sinners?" And this: "Is He a God of wrath or of love?—and how does this relate to homosexuality?"

From this book you will learn to love as God loves by understanding and sharing His views.

Do not be fooled by my simple words and short sentences. "Theology" is the study of God, and telling the story of God is deeply theological. In this book you will discover things not taught in seminary, yet I deliberately write in plain English at the eighth grade reading level. This is true of both theological and cultural terms used.

The gay world has many words to describe its various sexual preferences. To avoid confusion and to make the language simple, this book uses only two words: homosexual and gay—both used in a gender-neutral way.

Homosexual

I use the word "homosexual" to describe a person who experiences sexual attraction for someone of the same sex. Such an attraction fits the category of temptation. Temptation is not sin. Temptation that is given in to and acted upon is sin.

Many followers of Jesus endure tremendous same-sex attraction but never act upon that temptation. They practice celibacy just as Jesus did. They do not define their lives by their sexual orientation but rather transcend this temptation the same way an alcoholic does who says at the AA meeting, "Hi. My name is [insert name here], I am an alcoholic, and no alcohol has passed my lips in 37 years...."

I am not sure why such persons continue to identify themselves by either their beverage or their sexual preferences, but since they do, I respect and use their vocabulary.

Gay

I use the word "gay" for a person who practices homosexual behavior whether in defiance or ignorance regarding the Bible's clear teaching against this sin. Some of these individuals are militant and vocal advocates of the homosexual political agenda that includes gay marriage. Many others quietly ignore the publicity and merely indulge their desires in private.

Book I of this collection, *The Big Picture*, tells the story of God, a story that reveals why both homosexuals and gays desperately need you to show them the love that is of God. Book II, *The Love Picture*, gives many examples from the Bible of people who actively loved their homosexual and gay neighbors. Book III, *The Gay Picture*, summarizes the recent events making this book necessary and provides final instructions on how to love, and what the result of your loving is likely to be.

Introduction: The Hair Dresser

My pastor friend Brenda is an intentional friend to others. A few years ago she decides to get her hair done at a new place, and every visit she makes sure to schedule the same hair dresser in order to establish a new friendship.

Denny is an excellent hair dresser and makes interesting conversation. They talk about music, books, TV shows, movies, and occasionally share more serious moments.

Somewhere in the relationship Denny becomes aware that Brenda is lead pastor of a church that makes the news because of things they do for the community. He compliments her on the social awareness of her church.

Their conversations become increasingly personal. Now it is just weeks away from Easter, and Brenda asks him to attend church on this special occasion.

"No way!" Dennis says. "I don't do church. And besides, I can't commit myself weeks in advance of something. I don't know what I'll be doing then."

"Come on, now," Brenda teases. "You know you can't say that. I make an appointment with you every six weeks, I pay to sit in your chair for a couple of hours, and I give you a good tip. All I am asking is for you to come once, sit in a free chair, and clear an hour to listen to me talk. You don't ever have to come again if you don't want, and I will still keep coming here."

Another hairdresser laughs and says, "She's got ya, Denny!" He agrees, promising he will come, "Just once."

Dennis goes to church that Easter Sunday, and for nearly a year he never misses a Sunday except the week he is on vacation. Brenda keeps getting her hair done, and the conversations became more personal. He even does free haircuts at a church outreach event.

One Sunday morning Brenda preaches about Jesus being the Rock, the firm foundation, and invites people who know they need to plant their feet firmly on Jesus to come forward and have someone pray with them.

Brenda is thrilled when she moves to the next person in line and sees it is Denny. She takes his hand and asks what he wants to pray about. He says, "I want to commit my life to Christ this morning, and be baptized tonight!"

And that's what happens. A few weeks later, Brenda is at the salon again, and Denny is wearing his baptismal T-shirt, boldly emblazoned across the back, "I WILL NEVER BE THE SAME AGAIN."

As he begins to cut her hair, Brenda tells him how delighted she is to see him wearing the shirt. He says, "Oh, yeah...I wear it everywhere. It gives me a great opportunity to have the conversation with my friends about my life now and about accepting Christ. I just wore it to the Harbor (a local hangout) Friday night."

When she asks him what his friends say about his shirt and what he says in response, his eyes meet hers in the mirror. "I tell them I gave my life to Jesus and got baptized, and then...well, you did know I was gay, right?"

She replies, looking steadily back at him, "I didn't know, Denny—and I didn't think about it. I don't label people like that."

"Well, I am. I have always felt this was my identity. I thought you knew—everyone else does."

"So what do your friends think about your choice?"

They all say, "What does your church have to say about the fact that you're gay?"

With a lump in her throat, Brenda presses forward. "And what do you tell them?" The haircutting has completely stopped.

Denny says, "I tell them I don't know—that I have never heard my pastor talk about homosexuality. She tells us we are to love like Jesus, and look for our answers in God's Word. She says to read the Bible and ask God for our answers."

The lump doesn't get any smaller. "And do you read the Bible?"

"Yes."

"What do you think it says?"

"Oh, I think it is clear that God's plan is not for me to be a homosexual. That's why it took me so long to commit my life to Jesus. I knew that when I made this commitment to Him, I would never be able to have this kind of a relationship. It took me awhile to be able to do that. But," he continues, "See what I got?"

He holds up his hand, the left finger adorned with a beautiful silver ring. "I bought this ring for myself to signify my relationship with Christ—his commitment to me and my commitment to Him."

Brenda's eyes fill with tears and her heart with awe. It is a true conversion—one with dimensions and implications we rarely see.

*   *   *   *   *

Brenda doesn't generally think about people "that way," but many people do. Western civilization is now thoroughly sexualized—not unlike Ephesus in the first century where the sex goddess Artemis dominated the culture.

So this is a book about how to love your gay neighbor, friend, sibling, child, and co-worker. In many ways that love will show up in all the same ways as you love anybody else.

Perhaps you have heard about the five love languages—the ways of expressing love that come naturally to you. You can easily speak those languages to a gay person as well as to anyone, whether it is baking cookies (or any act of service), giving a gift, providing a shoulder massage (or any appropriate physical touch), speaking encouraging words (words of affirmation), or spending quality time together.

This book goes beyond such established social actions to equip you to love your gay neighbor in more profound ways. I'll share from the Bible a few things you should know about God, a few things you should know about love, and a few things you should know about homosexuality. Knowing these things will make you a better lover.

Since God IS love, let's begin with the story of God. In telling God's story, I quote from a new translation of the Bible called *The Voice* that uses many phrases in *italics* to clarify the meaning for modern readers. None of the *italics* in Bible quotes are added by me for emphasis—they are in the original.

Book I: The Big Picture

Chapter 1

The Story of God

Whenever you make new friends, one of the first things you want to hear is their story. What shaped them? What happened to them? Why do they have only one leg? What does that tattoo represent?

The purpose of worship in the gathered church is to rehearse the story of God. You can get to know God by hearing His story—often referred to as "salvation history"—and thereby understanding why His arm is so long, and where His attitudes and opinions come from.

If God comes across as angry in certain circumstances, you'll find out why. If He is loving and kind in other situations, you'll see His motives. If you perceive Him to be judge of the whole world, you'll recognize where He gets that authority.

You must get to know God well if you hope to love your gay neighbor the way God loves that neighbor. A summary of God's story will give you the big picture. The wise place to begin is to recognize that He exists:

The foolish are convinced deep down that there is no God. Their souls are polluted, and they commit gross injustice. Not one of them does good. From Heaven the one True God examines the earth to see if any understand *the big picture*, if any seek to know the True God. (Ps. 53:1-2)

The church year observes the story of God with Advent anticipating Christmas and the birth of Jesus followed by Epiphany celebrating his life, ministry, and teachings as recorded in the Gospels. Then comes Lent and the anticipation of his betrayal, execution by Romans, death and burial on Good Friday. Three days later is Easter and the celebration of his return from death, followed 40 days later by his Ascension into heaven. Pentecost and the permanent arrival of the Holy Spirit conclude the church year celebrating the story of God.

The whole story of the eternal God is longer than that, beginning with creation of the universe and the heavenly world. We know very little about this time-before-time, but one glimpse into the big picture happens after the disciples of Jesus are sent out to do missionary work. When they come back, they say to

Jesus in amazement, "Lord! When we use Your name, the demons do what we say!"

Jesus replies, "*I know.* I saw Satan falling from above like a lightning bolt" (Luke 10: 17-18). Isaiah gives a more detailed description:

My, how you've fallen from *the heights of* heaven! O morning star, son of the dawn! *What a star you were,* as you *menaced and* weakened the nations, but now you've been cut down, *fallen* to earth.

Remember how you said to yourself, "I will ascend to heaven—*reach higher and with more power*— and set my throne high above God's own stars?"

Remember how you thought you could be a god, saying: "I will sit *among them* at the mount of assembly in the northern heights. I will rise above the highest clouds and make myself like the Most High"?

Hah! Instead, you have sunk *like a stone* to where the dead abide. You've hit bottom of the bottommost pit. (Isa. 14:12-15)

Understanding this scene requires knowing who Jesus is and where He stood when He saw Satan fall. It requires appreciating that Jesus is One with the

Father and Holy Spirit and eternally exists. He created and sustains the universe. Satan was an executive officer in God's heavenly organization.

The Bible gives just a few tiny glimpses into the administrative structure of heaven, but three heavenly beings are identified by name: Michael, Lucifer, and Gabriel.

In direct service to the Father stands the most powerful warrior, Michael. Serving and worshiping with him are many cherubim or "winged guardians" of holy places who guard the entrance to Eden (Gen. 3:24) and the seat of mercy in the tabernacle and temple (Num. 7:89). They are the astonishing creatures with spinning wheels and four faces as described in Ezekiel 10.

In direct service to the Holy Spirit is the messenger Gabriel. Ten times he is named in the Bible, appearing to Daniel, Zacharias, the Virgin Mary, and Joseph. He represents the Holy Spirit, and with him are the seraphim that appear in Isaiah, Revelation, and probably at Pentecost although not named. Seraphim appear to humans as flaming creatures or tongues of fire.

In direct service to Jesus were Lucifer, Angel of Light, and a vast team of ministering spirits on the order of cherubim and seraphim. The short sentence from Jesus, "I saw Satan falling from above like a lightning bolt," is packed with profound personal meaning. We are told that a battle broke out in heaven:

Michael, along with his heavenly messengers, clashed against the dragon. The dragon and his messengers returned the fight, but they did not prevail and were defeated. *As a result,* there was no place left for them in heaven. So the great dragon, that ancient serpent who is called the devil and Satan, the deceiver of the whole world, was cast down to the earth along with his messengers. (Rev. 12:7-9)

The dragon's tail brushed one-third of the stars from the sky and hurled them down to the earth. The dragon crouched in front of the laboring woman, waiting to devour her child the moment it was born. (Rev. 12:4)

Casting Lucifer and his one-third of the heavenly beings out of heaven leaves a gaping hole in God's realm. The body of Jesus the Christ is eviscerated in heaven when all those who serve Him are cast out.

Who will serve Him now?

What is God's plan for filling the gaping hole in heaven? This brings us to Genesis:

> **God:** Now let Us conceive *a new creation*—humanity—*made* in Our image, *fashioned* according to Our likeness. And let *Us grant* them authority over all the earth— the fish in the sea and the birds in the sky, the domesticated animals and the *small* creeping creatures on the earth.
>
> So God did *just that.* He created humanity in His image, created them male and female. Then God blessed them and gave them *this directive*: "Be fruitful and multiply. Populate the earth. *I make you trustees of My estate,* so care for My creation and rule over the fish of the sea, the birds of the sky, and every creature that roams across the earth."
>
> And it happened *just as God said.* Then God surveyed everything He had made, savoring *its beauty and appreciating* its

goodness. Evening gave way to morning.

That was day six. (Gen. 1:26-310

On this sixth and final creation event, God's great plan to fill the place in heaven begins. He designs a people for Himself, made in His image. They are more beautiful than the Angel of Light—and that is saying a lot. Here is a fitting description:

You lived in Eden, God's garden. You were clothed in *magnificent splendor,* covered in jewels: Sardius, topaz, diamond, beryl, onyx, jasper, lapis lazuli, turquoise, and emerald. All the mountings were made of gold, prepared for you on the day you were created.

I anointed you the guardian *of the garden* and stationed you *at your post* to protect it. You were on *the divine mountain,* the holy mount of God. There you walked among the fiery stones. You were entirely pure from the day you were created, until wickedness *crept in and* was found in you.... *Polluted and* disgraced, I drove you off the mountain of God! I expelled you, O guardian protector, from the fiery stones.

Your heart swelled with pride because of your beauty *and talents. Your hunger for fame,* your thirst for glory corrupted your wisdom. (Ezek. 28:13-17)

Satan is the most magnificent creation—until God makes Adam and Eve. Satan begins his corruption of humanity with Eve, not because she is weak, but because he is jealous. She is more beautiful than he, and a more noble creation. He knows he *must* destroy this crowning creation of God, this one with greater power than he, for she can create *life!* And not just any life, but living, eternal, soulful beings in the image of God and destined to take Satan's place in heaven.

The Great Deceiver appears to win round one. Sin enters the world, and therefore death. Lucifer introduces the opposite of every God-like quality. Consider these opposites:

God is the creator of life, so Satan introduces death. In God's image, humanity is innocent, so Satan introduces sin to make them guilty. God gives power to His people to rule the earth, and Satan replaces power with fear. God honors His people with authority, and Satan reduces them to nakedness and shame.

You can begin to see Satan's pattern. He turns purity to pollution. He destroys what God creates. He substitutes violence for peace, sorrow for joy, and hatred for love.

God made humanity in His image; Satan hopes to unmake humanity into his image. So it should come as no surprise that humanity in its fallen state "naturally" does these works of Deception:

1. Pride makes a god of self in the place of God.
2. Worship focuses on idols rather than on God, even to the extent of sacrificing children to demonic gods.
3. Profanity dishonors God's name.
4. Earthly material gain displaces hope of heaven.
5. Children learn to despise their parents.
6. Killing and hatred proliferate.
7. Sexual perversions dominate the imagination.
8. Stealing and violence become the rule.
9. Deception and falsehood flourish.
10. Covetousness becomes a pandemic of greed.

All these Lucifer traits destroy the image of God in humanity. Sin and death take over the world. God says He is sorry He created humanity in the first place and uses a great flood to destroy all of them except faithful Noah and his family (see Genesis 6).

It takes Noah many years to build his salvation boat, and in all that time the world goes gaily on its way. God does not act quickly, but when the time comes to shut the door, He acts suddenly. His first method of washing away sin is with water.

After the flood God sets a rainbow in the sky as a symbol of His promise to never again destroy the Earth with water. That the modern gay movement adopts the rainbow as its symbol is a gesture of disrespect to the God of the firmament, a mockery by people who twist the symbol of His faithfulness into their symbol of defiance.

No matter: God promises next time to destroy the Earth by fire as He foreshadows in the destruction of Sodom.

Time passes following the flood, and God fights back against death-by-Satan when He calls out from among the fallen people the man Abraham. He chooses a people for Himself and calls them to live in His holy ways that can redeem Earth and in the end fill the hole in heaven where fallen servants of Jesus once stood.

To Moses, the descendant of Abraham, God gives Ten Commandments to empower them to win over Deception's lies (Exodus 20):

1. I am the Eternal your God. I led you out of Egypt and liberated you from lives of slavery *and oppression.* [3] You are not to serve any other gods before Me.
2. You are not to make any idol *or image of other gods.*
3. You are not to use My name for your own idle purposes.
4. You and your family are to remember the Sabbath Day; set it apart, and keep it holy.
5. You are to honor your father and mother.
6. You are not to murder.
7. You are not to commit adultery.
8. You are not to take what is not yours.
9. You are not to give false testimony against your neighbor.
10. You are not to covet what your neighbor has.

God establishes the law and His people build the tabernacle as God's second method of washing away sin—by blood sacrifice. Innocent animals are slain to cover the sins of the world.

The story of God continues into the New Testament; the second covenant. When it looks like Satan will win over the people of God, Jesus comes in person to save them. The drama is summarized in Revelation 12: 4-5, where the story continues after the dragon's tail brushes one-third of the heavenly beings to earth:

> The dragon crouched in front of the laboring woman, waiting to devour her child the moment it was born. She gave birth to a male child, who is *destined* to rule the nations with an iron scepter. *Before the dragon could bite and devour her son,* the child was whisked away and brought to God and His throne.

This child, of course, is Jesus known as Immanuel— God with us. In the wilderness temptations and in the Garden of Gethsemane, Satan tries to win over Jesus just as he won over Eve in the Garden of Eden. At the crucifixion he thinks he has won, for there the body of Christ is eviscerated on earth, just as it was in heaven when Satan and his followers were tossed out.

Then comes the resurrection! The penalty for sin is death, but Jesus—the sinless One—cannot be held by death. He rises from the grave, gives final instructions to His followers, and returns to heaven and God's throne.

The battle intensifies. Satan knows he is now in a tough spot. He knows his time is short. His plan now is to bring powerful deception on the people of earth by intensifying his counterfeits to every godly thing.

Since he failed to destroy Immanuel, he tries now to destroy Immanuel's people. He is trying to destroy YOU. Deception sells a cheap counterfeit of every gift from God. Consider this list:

Immanuel's Virtues:	Satan's Vices
Humility	Pride
Kindness	Envy
Self-control	Gluttony
Chastity	Lust/pornography
Patience	Anger
Liberality	Greed
Diligence	Sloth

Satan's vices listed above are known as the seven deadly sins. But they do not begin to touch the lengths he goes to in counterfeiting the Word of God. The seven classical virtues of Immanuel are shown below paired with a short list of the works of Deception:

Immanuel's Traits	Satan's Traits
Faith	Doubt
Hope	Despair
Love	Hate
Peace	War
Logic	Confusion
Sanity	Insanity
Wisdom	Foolishness

No doubt you have heard about the "mark of the beast" in Revelation 13:15-16 where it is ordered "that those who refuse to worship the image of the *first* beast must be killed, and the earth-beast mandates that all humans must carry a mark on their right hands or foreheads: both great and small, both rich and poor, both free and slave."

This mark is Satan's imitation of something God does with His people in Exodus 13:9 and those who grieve over sin in Ezekiel 9:4. In the end time heavenly messengers will again "seal the servants of our God *with a mark of ownership* on their foreheads" (Rev. 7:3). We see this mark for the last time in the final chapter of the Bible where those invited into the City of God "will be able to look upon His face, and His name will be written on their foreheads" (Rev. 22:4).

Choose your side now. Receive the authentic mark of God and there will be no place remaining on your forehead for the counterfeit mark of Satan's beast. A time is coming when—without Satan's mark—you won't be able to buy or sell in the marketplace (see Rev. 13:17), but that will be the least of your worries.

The story of God is the story of a perpetual war between Him and Satan—and the prize is humanity. The prize is you! They are fighting a cosmic battle over your eternal soul, and the souls of your neighbors. In Galatians 5:19-21 Paul describes how Satan's counterfeit works turn up in human behavior:

It's clear that our flesh entices us into practicing some of its most heinous acts: participating in corrupt sexual relationships, impurity, unbridled lust, idolatry, witchcraft, hatred, arguing, jealousy, anger, selfishness, contentiousness, division, envy *of others' good fortune,* drunkenness, drunken revelry, and other shameful vices *that plague humankind.* I told you this clearly before, and I only tell you again *so there is no room for confusion:* those who give in to these

ways will not inherit the kingdom of God.

God counters Satan by sending the Holy Spirit so that His people—in this life—can fight on the same side with God. Empowered by the Holy Spirit, we are on assignment to live in the way Paul describes in Galatians 5:22-25:

> The Holy Spirit produces a different kind of fruit: love, joy, peace, patience, kindheartedness, goodness, faithfulness, gentleness, and self-control. You won't find any law opposed to fruit like this. Those of us who belong to the Anointed One have crucified our old lives and put to death the flesh and all the lusts and desires that plague us. *Now* since we have chosen to walk with the Spirit, let's keep each step in perfect sync with God's Spirit.

Satan could not have anticipated the arrival of Jesus on earth to redeem humanity, but when he sees it, he fights Jesus with every weapon in his arsenal. Temptation in the wilderness. A disciple named Judas. Torment. Rejection. Crucifixion.

"I'll give you anything if you'll only bow down and worship me," Satan says. His motive remains ever the same—to claim Jesus' place in heaven for himself—and to prevent that heavenly void from being filled by you and me—and by all of those who repent of their sins and respond to the grace and new life Jesus offers.

Chapter 2
Deep Things of Satan

Satan is not all-knowing. He does not know the future. He probably did not expect Jesus to show up on earth; he could not have anticipated a sinless Jesus embracing and conquering death; the arrival of the Holy Spirit in a permanent way at Pentecost must have astonished that devil.

About the future, Satan only knows that his time is short. Desperate measures are necessary. But Satan is stuck. He has no new tactics. He is not the great Creator. He is merely the great Imitator. All his tools are revealed in Scripture—he has used them before.

Now that Jesus in human form has overcome death, now that the Holy Spirit makes it possible for people to overcome sin, now Satan realizes that achieving utter moral depravity for all humanity is his only task—his only hope—for keeping humanity from filling the space he vacated in heaven.

Satan's reality is summarized in a novel I wrote. Consider this conversation between my demon

Bwing and my protagonist Lord William (*The Shattered Urn* 60-61):

Bwing says, "Shaddai has His assistant Michael and all the cherubim and courtly beings that serve and worship Him; The Breath of Him has Gabriel and all the seraphim that do His bidding; Immanuel has nothing. Lucifer and those of us who served him rebelled and were forever severed. He wants to fill that hole."

"I see. And grace will somehow make that possible?"

Bwing replies, "No. We like the hole. We made it, and in the making, we hurt Him. We look for ways to hurt Him more. The Maker put life on Earth. Of all that He has made, He said the man and the woman are His best creation, for He made them in His own image. Like God, the man and the woman can also create life."

I say, "But so do the animals and all living things."

Bwing clarifies, "Animal lives do not have souls; they do not become everlasting creatures in the image of the Creator. Only a

34

man and a woman united can create another eternal being. He would repopulate the hole with them."

The Bible is clear that all sin is an outrage to God—it has the smell of Lucifer on it. The smallest of sin is enough to keep us out of the absolute holiness of the presence of God in heaven.

But it is a deception to conclude from this truth that all sins are equal. As stated in *The Shattered Urn*, "The only way forward in the mind of Deception is greater and greater depravity, for the bigger the sinner [he presumes], the lesser the grounds for mercy. He knows this by his own woeful experience when he was tossed out of the highest orbs of holiness" (41).

Thus, Satan works endlessly to push humanity toward greater and greater sin, and he knows the greatest sin of all would be the greatest counterfeit of God's most noble creation. The demon Bwing says as much in *The Shattered Urn*: "Marriage between a man and woman is the topmost creation of the One. Therefore, our topmost insult to the One is marriage between two men or two women. In this you see the ultimate achievement of Deception. No greater offense to the One is possible" (61).

Consider the importance of marriage in the Bible:

➤ The Bible begins with a man-and-woman wedding.

➤ Jesus performed His first miracle at a wedding blessing in Cana.

➤ The New Testament describes the Church as the *Body* of Christ, and as the *Bride* of Christ.

➤ The Bible ends with a great wedding banquet between Jesus and His chosen ones. The hole Lucifer left in heaven is filled as the Church—the bride of Christ—stands with Jesus in place of Lucifer and the one-third of the heaven's first population.

Marriage between a man and a woman made in God's image is the ultimate picture of God's restorative work in the world. In Revelation we see Jesus coming to earth to take His bride back to heaven. They will be His people; He will be their God. He will wipe away tears and both earth and heaven will be complete.

The hole in Heaven will be filled with the likes of you and me.

In these last days it is no wonder Satan is making his last desperate attack on marriage. He *must* destroy the image of God in the world. This is why homosexual marriage is the ultimate degradation of the image of God. Of all his counterfeits, this one matters most to Satan.

Now it is clear why the current assault on marriage is demonic. Fight against biblical marriage and you become the devil's pawn in the showdown of history.

In broad strokes, this is the story of God. And you play a part in that story.

If you are a person tempted with same-sex attractions, welcome to planet earth. This will be the landscape of your spiritual warfare. You must fight within yourself any temptations that your gay orientation may have imprinted on your psyche—because Jesus was tempted by Satan for 40 days in a wilderness not unlike yours (see Matt. 4 and Luke 4).

Satan tried but failed to destroy the moral integrity of God Himself in the form of Jesus. What can stop him from trying and succeeding at destroying the image of God in you? Satan seeks to consume and destroy you personally as well as the whole Body of Christ collectively. The way to defeat him—as Jesus did—will unfold for you as you work your way through this book.

Meanwhile, do not be deceived. God is not mocked. What you sow you will reap. So "Plant *a crop of* righteousness for yourselves, harvest *the fruit of* unfailing love, and break up your hard soil, because it's time to seek the Eternal until He comes and waters your fields with justice" (Hos. 10:12).

Satan's problem is that he has only experienced the wrath of God. He knows nothing of the grace of God. Because he has never repented, he has never known forgiveness. Because he is full of pride, he has never humbled himself before God to ask for salvation. This is the despair he knows; this is the despair he wants to imprint on you; this is the despair he perpetrates on the world today in his battle for gay marriage.

The way for the Church to win this battle is for each of us individually to love our gay neighbors through the power of the Holy Spirit. As we do this, Satan will lose one person at a time as each one experiences the grace of God.

Capturing in words the glory of such grace is impossible. John Bunyan attempted it in *The Holy War* and I have borrowed it in *The Shattered Urn* where the deceived ones of Havilah cannot believe all that the forgiveness and grace of God entails. They go to their execution expecting to die, but because of their sincere repentance, God executes grace instead of justice. Here is their report of that experience:

> We went down to the camp in black but come back arrayed in robes of white linen. We went down to the camp adorned with the hangman's noose and come back in necklaces of gold. We went down to the camp with our feet in fetters but come back with our steps unhampered. We went also to the camp looking for death and come back with assurance of life. We went down with heavy hearts but come back again with a clutch of merry-makers playing pipe and tabor before us. We looked for nothing but the axe and the block, but behold! Joy and gladness, comfort and consolation, and melodious tones attend us. (*SU* 91)

To see past Deception—
To repent—
To receive the grace of God—no matter how great your sin—is to step back into Eden and

experience fellowship with God. In this fellowship among believers you can become your best creative self in this life as well as in the life to come.

To receive the grace of God is to become one of the people God has chosen to win the ultimate battle over Satan in the new heaven and new earth where holiness and righteousness prevail—where God will wipe every tear from your eyes—and where you will live and reign with Jesus forever.

The concluding words of *The Shattered Urn* say it this way: "We have known Him, Immanuel. We have seen His glory, the glory of the One and only Son of Shaddai, full of grace and truth. We are filled with the Breath of Him, and we write these things so that you too can overcome Deception by knowing Him. In so doing, you will live this life to the full even as it prepares you for the life that is to come" (222).

Here is a picture of that life which is to come: you and all the true Church, the Body of Jesus the Anointed One, with Him and surrounded by God the Father, the Holy Spirit, and all the ministering spirits of heaven, celebrating in a place where the will of God is always done.

From God's all-knowing point of view, the purpose of your life and of all humanity is to love God and enjoy Him forever. You are meant to fill the hole left in heaven by Lucifer and that damned one-third of the former heavenly host.

From Satan's point of view, the purpose of your life and of all humanity is to obliterate the image of God and profane His name in every conceivable way.

Telling the story of God and knowing the deep things of Satan make it clear why homosexual practices including gay marriage are Satan's ultimate ploy to profane the image of God.

*   *   *   *   *

Now that you know a bit of God's story, you understand why you want to be on His side. You see what He expects of you. You comprehend the magnitude of the Holy War. You know what is at stake—for both you and for your neighbor.

What is at stake for you is the same as was true of Ezekiel. Here is what the Eternal One said to him:

Eternal One: Son of man, I have appointed you a sentry for the people of Israel. Listen to what I say, then deliver My warning to them. If I send this message to a wicked person—"You will die"—but then you fail to warn him or help him to reconsider his wickedness so that he may not die, then he will die as a result of his evil *deeds. It will be your fault for not warning him.* His blood will be on your hands. But if you do forewarn a wicked person *and give him My message,* and yet he does not change his wicked thoughts and actions, then he will die as a result of his evil *deeds.* But you will have saved your own life *by doing what I directed.* Or again, when a righteous person turns his back on righteousness and falls into evil, then I will place a stumbling block before him, and he will surely die *as well.* Since you haven't alerted him, he will die for his evil ways. None of the righteous things he did will be remembered, and I will hold you responsible for his death. But if you do forewarn a righteous person not to give in to sin, and he does not sin, he will certainly live because he listened to your warning, and you will have saved your own life *by doing what I directed.* (Ezek. 3:17-21)

God is saying here that we are responsible to love our neighbors. That love is expressed in all the ways we will discuss in this book, and especially when we let them know that what they are doing will one day get them killed—an eternal death. We should be as motivated to share with them the message of the Bible as we would be motivated to snatch them out of the path of a speeding truck. Or as Jude 23 says, "Pursue those who are singed by the flames *of God's wrath,* and bring them safely *to Him.*"

When you do this snatching, some neighbors will be offended. Others will look up, recognize the consequences of staying where they are, and step into the light where the truck can't go. You are responsible for them in either case.

To love in this way is terrifying, and you cannot do it alone. You need all the wisdom, patience, and timing that only the Holy Spirit can provide. Getting to that place can only be accomplished through prayer. The next chapter shows you how to pray in a particular way in order to prepare the way of the Lord into your gay neighbor's life.

Chapter 3
Pray Against Belial

John, the closest friend of Jesus, speaks the solution to all the longings of the homosexual population. He lovingly addresses the big gay lie that claims homosexual behavior is normal and should be acceptable in the Church:

> If we go around bragging, "We have no sin," then we are fooling ourselves and are strangers to the truth. But if we own up to our sins, God shows that He is faithful and just by forgiving us of our sins and purifying us from the pollution of all the bad things we have done. If we say, "We have not sinned," then we depict God as a liar and *show that* we have not let His word find its way into our hearts. (1 John 1:8-10)

In the same letter, John clearly explains the alternative to homosexual and any other sinful lifestyle:

> Everyone who lives a life of habitual sin is living in moral anarchy. That's what sin is.

You realize that He came to eradicate sins, that there is not the slightest bit of sin in Him. The ones who live in *an intimate relationship with* Him do not persist in sin, but anyone who persists in sin has not seen and does not know the real Jesus.

Children, don't let anyone pull one over on you. The one doing the right thing is just imitating Jesus, the Righteous One. The one persisting in sin belongs to the diabolical one, who has been all about sin from the beginning. That is why the Son of God came into our world: to destroy the plague of destruction inflicted *on the world* by the diabolical one.

Everyone who has been born into God's family avoids sin *as a lifestyle* because the genes of God's children come from God Himself. Therefore, a child of God can't live a life of persistent sin. (1 John 3:4-9)

The Bible is so very clear, no further discussion is necessary. The Church must see that to ordain gay clergy or permit members to persist in homosexual practices does fierce violence to the Body of Christ. No greater heresy has ever threatened the Church.

At the same time, the Church must lovingly embrace and nurture individuals who experience same-sex attractions. They need help in waging spiritual warfare against these evils the same as does the heterosexual who must fight sexual temptation.

Everyone has some cross to bear, some form of sin that comes easily. The essence of the godly life is the daily practice of transcending whatever that temptation may be, whether that person is an alcoholic, swindler, liar, or exhibits any other quality condemned by Scripture as sinful.

The beginning point is to recognize the need for such grace. You are loving your gay neighbor whenever you affirm that grace from God abounds to anyone who acknowledges a behavior as sin and repents.

You are *not* loving your gay neighbor when you and your social group branded "church" embrace and propagate the lie that homosexual *behavior* should be recognized as acceptable. The loving message is to urge your gay acquaintances to repent, turn from their wicked ways, and abandon their pride of worshiping themselves as god.

Astonishing actualization transpires in the lives of those who abandon their will to God, invite Him to control their lives, and devote their energies toward becoming all they were created to be rather than following their lower instincts and becoming twisted into all that the Un-creator longs to un-make of them.

When you reach a deep level of friendship so that direct communication is possible, it is time to lovingly say something like the following to your gay friend: An upward path and a downward path lie before you. Whether you believe it today or wait to experience it later, the alternative to the upward path of repentance and obedience is the downward path prophesied to end with the devil and his angels in a lake of fire (prepared by God in his all-knowing comprehension of best practices) to eradicate evil and make the coming new world a safe place for holiness, without which no person will see God.

Some will mock you for sharing a "turn or burn" message. Yet the actual biblical prophecy about a future action of Jesus reads as follows:

> It is done! I am the Alpha and the Omega,
> the beginning and the end. I will see to it
> that the thirsty drink freely from the
> fountain of the water of life. To the victors
> will go this inheritance: I will be their God,
> and they will be My children. *It will not be so*

for the cowards, the faithless, the
sacrilegious, the murderers, the sexually
immoral, the sorcerers, the idolaters, and all
those who deal in deception. They will
inherit *an eternity in* the lake that burns
with fire and sulfur, which is the second
death. (Rev. 21:6-8)

Notice that cowards are mixed right in there with homosexuals as fuel for the lake of fire. This is a good reason for setting aside your cowardice and taking steps now to love your gay neighbor.

The Apostle Paul puts the issue of homosexuality into proper context, including instructions on how to overcome this—or any other—temptation:

It's clear that our flesh entices us into
practicing some of its most heinous acts:
participating in corrupt sexual
relationships, impurity, unbridled lust,
idolatry, witchcraft, hatred, arguing,
jealousy, anger, selfishness,
contentiousness, division, envy *of others'*
good fortune, drunkenness, drunken revelry,
and other shameful vices *that plague*
humankind. I told you this clearly before,
and I only tell you again *so there is no room*

for confusion: those who give in to these ways will not inherit the kingdom of God.

The Holy Spirit produces a different kind of fruit: *unconditional* love, joy, peace, patience, kindheartedness, goodness, faithfulness, gentleness, and self-control. You won't find any law opposed to fruit like this. Those of us who belong to the Anointed One have crucified our old lives and put to death the flesh and all the lusts and desires that plague us. (Gal. 5:19-24)

A legitimate prayer in these times is that a great spiritual awakening will sweep over America and the entire world, giving us a tiny taste of that coming Kingdom when the will of God will be done on earth just as it is done in heaven.

An important detail of this prayer is to pray against the demon Belial. Why pray against Belial in particular? Because it is an extremely powerful fiend tasked with advancing homosexual behavior throughout the world. [I use the pronoun "it" referring to "Belial" as it is a fallen demon without race or gender.]

Do as I did when I walked around my house, my neighborhood, my workplace, and my church praying against the demon Belial. Pray to cast it out of each place. Set a spiritual hedge around those properties so that Belial will have no influence here, and that people who enter these places will be free from its lies.

How is praying against Belial significant? Followers of Jesus have been given authority to cast out demons, and this is the only power by which the invasion of the demonic into the Church can be held in check.

The Hebrew term *belial* is translated "worthless" or "without value" and appears 27 times in the Hebrew Scriptures, 15 times to indicate worthless people including idolaters (Deut. 13:13), the homosexual men of Gibeah (Judg. 19:22, 20:13), and Nabal, and Shimei, the sexually perverted sons of Eli (1 Sam. 2:12).

New Testament instructions on dealing with Belial are explicit:

Don't develop partnerships with those who are not followers of Jesus' teachings. For what real connection can exist between righteousness and rebellion? How can light participate in darkness? What harmony can exist between the Anointed and Belial? Do the faithful and the faithless have anything in common? Can the temple of God find common ground with idols? Don't you see that we house the temple of the living God within us? *Remember when* He said, "I will make My home with them and walk among them. I will be their God, and they will be My people. So then turn away from them, turn away and leave *without looking back*," says the Lord. "Stay away from anything unclean, *anything impure,* and I will welcome you. And I will be for you as a father, and you will be for Me as sons and daughters," says the Lord Almighty! (2 Cor. 6:14-18)

Belial is a spiritual power stronger than anyone except the Holy Spirit and that powerful messenger of God, Michael, and his holy ones who fight on behalf of holiness.

Your gay neighbors are stalked by the demon Belial. They will never escape its clutches unless you intercede for them with Holy Spirit power. When you do pray in such a way, you are following instructions given in Galatians 6:2 "Shoulder each other's burdens, and then you will live as the law of the Anointed teaches us."

Be warned: Belial may shift his attack from your gay neighbor to you. And you are no stronger to resist it than is your neighbor. So pray for yourself as well, for now you are on the front lines of battle.

God wants to use you to save your gay neighbors, relatives, and friends from the destruction set for them at the hand of Belial. Pray against Belial in all the places where you live, work, and play so that you will see the day prophesied by Isaiah: "They will say of Me, 'Only by the Eternal One *shall I see things through. Only by God* shall I go with integrity and strength *through life.*' Now all those who burned with anger against God will come to Him and be shamed" (Isa. 45:24).

In praying for the fulfillment of such ancient prophesies as this one, you join in spiritual warfare with saints throughout the ages. You must also join them in patience, as in "I wait for the Eternal—my soul awaits rescue—and I put my hope in His transforming word. My soul waits for the Lord to break into the world more than night watchmen expect the break of day, even more than night watchmen expect the break of day" (Psa. 130:5-6).

Book II: The Love Picture

Chapter 4

A Definition of Love

You've heard the word "love" used in so many ways, how can you possibly know what people mean by it? Am I saying you should love your gay neighbor the same way you love your coffee, your iPhone, your rose bush, your job, your favorite music, steak and lobster...?

Word definitions shift over time, so let's begin in the city of Corinth, the love capital of the world at the time when the Apostle Paul writes his famous definition of love for them. This trading city in Greece, located on a narrow strip of land between the Aegean and Ionian Seas, teams with people who define love as sexual activity.

The people receiving Paul's letter live in the shadow of a temple devoted to *Aphrodite*, a Greek goddess whose magical girdle arouses sexual desire. The temple features 1,000 *hierodouloi*—female prostitutes. A magnificent stone sculpture of Aphrodite stands in the Toledo Museum of Art. I have stood nose-to-nose with that human-sized, stone image and contemplated her many charms.

Corinth defines love differently from the Bible. Paul takes on the task of explaining the good news of Jesus to the people of this highly sexualized town. His creative approach is to introduce a new definition of love that no doubt astounds the Corinthians:

> What if I speak in the *most elegant* languages of people or in the *exotic* languages of the heavenly messengers, but I live without love? Well then, anything I say is like the clanging of brass or a crashing cymbal.

> What if I have the gift of prophecy, am blessed with knowledge and insight to all the mysteries, or what if my faith is strong enough to scoop a mountain *from its bedrock*, yet I live without love? If so, I am nothing.

> I could give all that I have to feed the poor, I could surrender my body to be burned *as a martyr*, but if I do not live in love, I gain nothing *by my selfless acts.*

> Love is patient; love is kind. Love isn't envious, doesn't boast, *brag, or strut about.*

There's no arrogance in love; it's never rude, crude, or indecent—it's not self-absorbed. Love isn't easily upset. Love doesn't tally wrongs or celebrate injustice; but truth— *yes, truth*—is love's delight! Love puts up with anything and everything that comes along; it trusts, hopes, and endures no matter what.

Love will never become obsolete. Now as for the prophetic gifts, they will not last; unknown languages will become silent, and the gift of knowledge will no longer be needed. Gifts of knowledge and prophecy are partial at best, *at least for now,* but when the perfection *and fullness of God's kingdom* arrive, all the parts will end.

When I was a child, I spoke, thought, and reasoned in childlike ways *as we all do.* But when I became a man, I left my childish ways behind. For now, we can only see a dim and blurry picture of things, as when we stare into polished metal. I realize that everything I know is only part of the big picture. But one day, *when Jesus arrives,* we will see clearly, face-to-face. In that day, I will fully know just as I have been wholly known *by God.*

But now faith, hope, and love remain; these three *virtues must characterize our lives.* The greatest of these is love. (1 Cor. 13)

Paul begins by saying eloquent language is just noise unless spoken with love. He says spiritual gifts are without value unless exercised with love. Verse three says selfless acts gain nothing if not done with love as the motive.

The first three verses discuss things that are good but useless if not carried out in a loving manner. Verses four through seven give the details on how to do such things lovingly. They are instructions on how to love your gay neighbor:

1. Be patient with this person (no matter how you are treated in return).

2. Be kind to this person (no matter how you are treated in return).

3. Do not envy this person for any reason.

4. Do not give your neighbor any reason to envy you by bragging, showing off, or being arrogant.

5. Do not be rude, crude, or indecent in the presence of this neighbor.

6. Do not be easily upset by anything this neighbor does.

7. Do not keep track of wrong things this neighbor does.

8. Delight in the truth as you trust in God, maintain high hopes about the future, and patiently endure any present inconveniences.

Verses eight through ten show that loving in this way is not trendy or temporary; such love is the only thing with life-long endurance. Love defines the mature follower of Jesus, as illustrated in verses eleven and twelve: right now we have only a dim idea of how important love is. However, the day is coming when we will see Jesus face-to-face. That's when we will fully understand that loving our gay neighbor has more value than any other way we can possibly spend our time, resources, and talents.

The three virtues of faith, hope, and love matter a lot, and love matters most. So start loving your gay neighbor!

Problem: You are not naturally disposed to love in this way. So loving others must begin with a prayer—for yourself. Here is one way to phrase such a prayer:

Dear Lord Jesus, here I am. Again today (or perhaps for the first time) I give my life to You. As Your child, my desire is to please You. But as You know, I live in an evil world. Loving others is not in my nature. I am by nature selfish. I have no power to love the way You have taught in the letter Paul wrote to those followers of Jesus in Corinth. They certainly had no such power, either.

Please give me Your love today. Fill me with Your Holy Spirit. Only then can I perfectly love You. Only then can I do a good job of representing Your holy name. Please fill me to overflowing with Your love so that it will spill over into the lives of others. So be it!

Chapter 5
Abraham Loves His Gay Neighbors

Paul defines love as something you do with your mind. He mentions nothing about how it feels for your body. To uncover some of the emotions involved, let's start with Abraham. This noble patriarch models how to *do* love with regard to his gay neighbors.

Abraham is known for obeying God's instructions—no matter what. God tells him to leave his home and move to a strange new place. So Abraham moves.

Genesis 13 reports that Abraham settles in a place called Canaan, and then later moves to Hebron, pitching his tent near the oaks of Mamre. His nephew, Lot, moves east and puts down roots in the town called Sodom. Genesis 13:13 says, "Now *you need to know that* the people of *the city of* Sodom were quite wicked—utterly defiant toward God."

The wickedness of his neighbors does not prevent Abraham from taking actions that show he loves them. When the military forces of Sodom and

Gomorrah are defeated and all their possessions taken by an enemy, the adversary also takes Lot as prisoner along with everything he owns.

Abraham takes particular interest in this war when it affects his own family. The Bible gives this report:

As soon as Abram heard that his nephew had been taken prisoner, he gathered a company of his *most reliable and* best-trained men (there were 318 of them, all born in his household) and pursued the enemy as far *north* as Dan.

When he caught up with them, Abram divided up his men, *surrounded the enemy,* and attacked them during the night. He and his soldiers crushed the invaders and pursued any survivors all the way to Hobah, north of Damascus.

After the battle Abram recovered all the spoils *the enemy had taken* and brought them back *with him.* He rescued his nephew Lot and brought him back, along with his goods; there were other captives, too, including some women whom he rescued" (Gen. 14:11-16).

Abraham's loving act of war restores his nephew and his neighbors. To show his approval of this loving act, God sends his priest-king Melchizedek from Jerusalem to serve Abraham a meal of bread and wine. He also speaks a special blessing over Abraham:

> **King Melchizedek:** May Abram be blessed by the Most High God, Creator of the heavens and earth. Blessing *and honor* to the Most High God, who has *clearly* delivered your enemies into your hands!
>
> Abram gave the priest-king a tenth of all *of the captured goods he was bringing back with him.* (Gen. 14:19-20)

The king of Sodom then generously said to Abraham, "Give me the people, and you can take all of the spoils for yourself." Here is Abraham's reply:

> I have pledged a solemn oath to the Eternal One—the Most High God, Creator of the heavens and earth. I promised that I would not keep *any shred of* what belongs to you—not a thread *of a garment* or a strap of a sandal. That way you could never take credit for any wealth of mine. I will take nothing except the food my men have eaten.

As for the men who fought with me—Aner, Eshcol, and Mamre—let them take their shares, *but I will take nothing more.* (Gen. 14:22-24)

The king of Sodom and his people are without doubt gay. The Bible makes this clear a few chapters later. Yet Abraham treats the king of Sodom with utmost dignity, honor, and respect. At the same time, he shares about his deep faith in God and his commitment to obeying God in every detail of his life. In so doing, he shows love to his gay neighbor.

Some years pass, but Abraham is still living near the oaks of Mamre when God appears to him in the guise of three men. The entire story is printed here so you can experience firsthand how strenuously Abraham pleads with God not to destroy his gay neighbors:

Eternal One *(to the other two men)*: I wonder if I should hide from Abraham what I am about to do. After all, Abraham will become *the father of* a great and powerful nation, and all the other nations of the earth will find their blessing in him. I have chosen him *for a reason, namely* that he will carefully instruct his children and his household *to keep themselves strong in relationship to Me and* to walk in My ways by doing what is *good and* right in the world and by showing *mercy and* justice *to all others. I know he will uphold his end of the covenant,* so that he can ensure My promises to him will be fulfilled and upheld as well.

I have heard terrible things—urgent and outraged calls *for help*—coming from *the cities of* Sodom and Gomorrah, and their sin has become a serious problem. I must go down and see *for Myself* whether the outcries against them that My ears have heard are really true. If not, I will know.

At this point the men turned and headed toward Sodom while Abraham remained standing before the Eternal One. Then Abraham approached Him *solemnly and pled for the city.*

Abraham *(to God)*: *God,* would You really sweep away the people who do what is right along with those who are wicked? What if there were 50 upright people within the city? Would You still wipe the place out and not spare it on behalf of the 50 upright people who live there? Surely it can't be Your nature to do something like that—to kill the right-living along with those who act wickedly, to consign the innocent to the same fate as the guilty. It is inconceivable to me that You, *my God,* would do anything like that! Will not the *"Merciful and Loving Judge"* of all the earth do what is just?

Eternal One: If I find 50 good and true people in the city of Sodom, *I give you My word* I will spare the entire city on their behalf.

Abraham *(emboldened)*: Look, I know I am just *a human being,* scooped from the dust and ashes *of the earth,* but if I might implore You, Lord, a bit further: What if the city lacked 5 of those 50 right-living people? *What then?* Would You destroy the entire city because it lacked those 5?

Eternal One: I won't destroy the city if I find 45 *good and true people* there.

Abraham *(persisting)*: Suppose 40 are found there.

Eternal One: I won't destroy the city for the sake of 40.

Abraham: Please don't be angry, Lord, *at my boldness*. Let me ask this: What if You found 30 there *who are good and true*?

Eternal One: I will not do it, even if I find only 30 there.

Abraham: Since I have implored the Lord this far, *may I ask:* What if there were 20?

Eternal One: For the sake of 20, I will not destroy the city.

Abraham: Please don't be angry, Lord, *at my boldness.* Let me ask this just once more: suppose only 10 are found?

Eternal One: For the sake of only 10, I still will not destroy it.

At this point the Eternal ended the conversation with Abraham and went on His way, and Abraham returned to his home. (Gen. 18:17-33)

This amazing discussion between the Lord and Abraham raises many interesting questions. Does Abraham love these people more than God does? Certainly not, for God *is* love. Does God know more about the depraved condition of these people than Abraham knows? Certainly, for God is all-knowing. Is God too hasty in punishing evil? Obviously not, for He says, "I must go down and see *for Myself* whether the outcries against them that My ears have heard are really true."

People pray about many things. The most loving and unselfish kind of prayer is when we plead with God for the sake of someone else. We beg Him to save them, to spare them grief or sorrow or trouble or pain or loss. Or death.

And God most certainly respects the prayers of this man Abraham about whom He has just said, "I have chosen him *for a reason, namely* that he will carefully instruct his children and his household *to keep themselves strong in relationship to Me and* to walk in My ways by doing what is *good and* right in the world and by showing *mercy and* justice *to all others*"(Gen. 18:19).

In the same way and for the same reasons, Jesus respects our intercessory prayers. Hebrews 7 recalls the story of Abraham and Melchizedek, explaining that through Jesus "God has now introduced a new and better hope" because "Jesus holds His priesthood permanently because He lives His resurrected life forever. From such a vantage, He is able to save those who approach God through Him for all time because

He will forever live to be their advocate *in the presence of God*" (Heb. 7:19, 24-25).

As our advocate before God, Jesus is "devoted to God, blameless, pure, *compassionate toward but* separate from sinners, and exalted by God to the highest place of honor" (Heb. 7:26).

Jesus is always praying for those He loves. While dying on the cross he says, "It is finished," and completes His work on earth. When He ascends into heaven, He begins a new work there. We are told in Romans 8:34 that "Jesus the Anointed was raised to sit at the right hand of God where He pleads on our behalf."

You are invited to join Jesus there at the right hand of God to intercede for your gay neighbors. Ephesians 2:6 informs us that "He raised us up with Him and seated us in the heavenly realms with *our beloved* Jesus the Anointed, *the Liberating King.*" Colossians 3:1 adds, "So *it comes down to this:* since you have been raised with the Anointed One, *the Liberating King,* set your mind on heaven above. The Anointed is there, seated at God's right hand."

The profound reality is that we who are raised with Jesus are already seated with Him at the right hand of God. Our task there is to join with Him in the work of pleading with God on behalf of those we love. This is the ultimate way to become Christ-like—and Abraham-like. We can devote our lives to praying passionately for the benefit of our gay neighbors.

Abraham's prayer is not answered in the way he hopes; ours may not be either. But unanswered prayers are not wasted prayers if they mold us into people who are more like Jesus. And the potential benefit to those we love cannot be measured.

Abraham prays urgently, sensing that time is short for his neighbors in Sodom. No doubt he also fears his nephew Lot and his family will be destroyed with the town.

However, just as he would do again in the future with the followers of Moses in Egypt, God is very discriminating—able to distinguish between the wicked and the righteous, destroying one and saving the other—as is clear in the next chapter.

Chapter 6

Lot Loves His Gay Neighbors

Abraham's nephew Lot is sitting at the gate of Sodom when the two heavenly messengers arrive that evening. This gate seat is a position of honor and respect. It shows that he has high standing among the men of Sodom.

We know from 2 Peter 2:8 that Lot is "a person who did what was right in God's eyes and who was distressed by the immorality *and the lawlessness* of the society around him. Day after day, the sights and sounds of their lawlessness were like daggers into that good man's soul."

Lot is anxious—just like his Uncle Abraham—to be an advocate for this city. Read the story carefully to appreciate the lengths to which Lot goes to save his gay neighbors:

> When Lot saw [the two heavenly messengers], he went out to meet them and bowed low, his face touching the ground.
>
> **Lot:** Please, my lords, take time to come into your servant's house to spend the night and

wash your feet. Then you can rise early and be on your way.

Messengers: No, we will be *fine* spending the night in the city square.

But Lot persisted *and urged them to come home with him and enjoy his hospitality.* They agreed finally and came with Lot to his house. Lot prepared a huge meal for them, served with unleavened bread, and they ate *until they were full.* But before they could lie down *to rest for the night,* the men of the city—that is, the men of Sodom, young and old alike, every last one of them—surrounded the house and called out to Lot.

Men of Sodom: Where are the men who came *with you* to your house tonight? *We saw them go in with you!* Bring them out here. We want to have sex with them!

Lot slipped out of the door to address the men, shutting it *firmly* behind him.

Lot: *Look,* I beg you, brothers, don't do this. Don't sink to this level of depravity! Look—I have two daughters. Both are virgins. How about this: I'll bring them out for you instead. You can do with them as you please. But please don't do anything to these men. They are my guests. They deserve the protection of my home.

Men of Sodom: Get out of the way, man! (to each other) Look, this guy came to our city as a stranger. *He's not one of us,* and yet he thinks he has the right to judge *all of us!* (to Lot) *You better watch out, or* we'll treat you far worse than we will your guests!

They came at Lot and pushed him hard against the door until it was about to break. Just then the men inside reached out and pulled Lot into the house with them, shutting the door *securely to block the men of Sodom out.* Then the *heavenly* messengers struck all of the men pressing at the door with blindness—both young and old alike. *It wasn't long before* they exhausted themselves *blindly* groping for the door.

Messengers *(to Lot):* Do you have anyone else here in the city—sons-in-law, sons, daughters, or any other members of your family—*whom you want to save?* If so, you need to get them out of here right now! We are going to destroy this place. Because of the immense outcry the Eternal One has received regarding the depravity of this city, the Eternal has sent us here to destroy it.

So Lot went out and found the young men who had pledged to marry his daughters.

Lot: Get up, and get out of this place. The Eternal One is going to destroy the city!

But his sons-in-law thought he was kidding *and wouldn't budge*. At dawn, the heavenly messengers urged Lot to action again.

Messengers: *Lot,* you need to get up and take your wife and two daughters out of here. Otherwise you will be consumed along with the rest of the city.

But Lot kept procrastinating, so the two heavenly messengers grabbed him, his wife, and his two daughters by the hand. They took them outside the city, *a safe distance away,* because the Eternal decided to show mercy to Lot *and his family.* As they were leading them *to safety,* one of the messengers gave this instruction:

Messenger: *Now run!* Run for your lives! Don't look back or stop anywhere in the plain. Head for the hills, or you'll die along with everyone else.

Lot: My lords, no. I realize you have shown me great kindness and favored me by saving my life. But please—I can't run that far. The devastation will surely catch up with me, and I'll die anyway. Look, over there is a city. It's not too far. I could escape there. It's just a little one. Please, let me go there instead. Then my life will surely be saved!

Messenger: Look, as a favor to you, I won't destroy the little city you're talking about. But hurry now; escape there, because I can't do anything until you arrive there safely!

Because of this, the little city *Lot escaped to* was called Zoar, *which means, "little."*

Lot *and his family* arrived in Zoar just as the sun was coming up. Then the Eternal One rained sulfur and fire from out of the heavens onto Sodom and Gomorrah. He destroyed both cities, along with the other villages and towns in the valley and all of the people who lived there—even the vegetation *was wiped out*! But Lot's wife *never made it; she* lagged behind her husband and looked back—*despite the messenger's advice*—and turned into a pillar of salt.

Meanwhile, Abraham rose early in the morning and went out to the place where he had stood at *the feet of* the Eternal One. He looked down toward where Sodom and Gomorrah *had been.* He looked up and down the valley, and *everywhere he looked* clouds of smoke were billowing up—*black,* like smoke from a giant furnace. Now *you know the story of* how God destroyed the cities of the valley, but remembered Abraham *and His covenant with him.* So He sent Lot out of the destruction—out of the cities where he had been living. (Gen. 19:1-29)

I visited Jordan and stood on the shores of the Dead Sea just a few miles north of where the best archaeological evidence suggests Sodom was probably located. At its surface the Dead Sea is 1,300 feet below sea level—the lowest place on earth. Standing at such a low place and knowing its low history is terrifying. It gives me a sense of the mighty power of God. The One who created and sustains the universe can surely melt such a town and cast it into the depths of the sea.

We are not told the motives behind the love that both Abraham and Lot show to the people of Sodom. But it is clear they do everything they possibly can to warn and protect their neighbors. Lot even offers them his daughters—perhaps a desperate effort to get them to change their sexual preference, but more likely conclusive evidence of their depravity. Even the men engaged to these two women show no interest in them and choose to remain in the city with their gay friends.

Abraham gets up early the next morning to see whether his prayer of intercession is answered—to see whether the cities still survive. We don't know his expectations, but we do know he has long experience with God. He simply obeys God, regardless of the consequences. And he has a deep humility about himself and utmost respect for God.

On this hazy morning, everywhere Abraham looks he sees devastation—black smoke as if from a giant furnace. I wonder how he felt in that moment. He might have collapsed to his knees in amazement, plugging his nose to quench the sulfuric smell. Here is the sort of prayer he might have offered:

Dear Lord, Your ways are beyond my understanding. Why would You compel me to pray so diligently for such doomed people? (I could have been shearing sheep or taking a nap.) And why did You spare me—and Lot? We are sinners as well. And why have You blessed me so much? You have said it is because I am to be a blessing to others. And I have been. I rescued these people from their enemies. I returned all their goods. I could have ruled that city, but instead I gave back to the king of Sodom all his people and all their stuff.

I risked my life for them, not to mention the lives of all my employees. It looks as if all my loving—all my justice—all my compassion is wasted. What kind of God are You that You would ask me to do justice— and then You do punishment? Just who do You think You are!

Two things are incomprehensible to Abraham, three he cannot fully grasp: the magnitude of the holiness of God that does not tolerate sin, the magnitude of the evil that opposes God so that from time to time He must wipe out such evil for the sake of future generations, and the mystery of the purposes of God with humanity.

By contrast, these days you see propaganda on some church signs saying things like "God does not discriminate; neither do we." Such slogans are not only logical fallacies—false premises leading to false conclusions—they trivialize the incomprehensible. They put themselves in place of the Judge of All by judging His actions. They make themselves God. Even as they pray eloquently and perform liturgies graciously, they embody the desires of Lucifer.

By contrast, Paul writes in Romans 11:33, "*We cannot wrap our minds around* God's wisdom and knowledge! Its depths can never be measured! We cannot understand His judgments or explain the mysterious ways that He works!"

Paul then alludes to Isaiah 40:13: "Who can fathom the mind of the Lord? Or who can claim to be His advisor?" He asks along with Job, "Who can give to God in advance so that God must pay him back?" (Job 41:11).

Paul concludes, "For all that exists originates in Him, comes through Him, and is moving toward Him; so give Him the glory forever" (Rom. 11:36).

Paul's doxology on the majesty of God is reflected in Abraham's humility before this hard-to-explain Eternal One who calls him to obedience. Although his prayers are not answered in the way he hopes, you can be sure Abraham is still very thankful to have prayed those prayers of intercession for his neighbors in Sodom. He has already rescued them once, and now he is not to blame for their destruction. He has done everything in his power to love them to the end.

One lesson to take from this story is that God's servants pray for their gay neighbors—the ultimate act of love.

Chapter 7

Love in the Jordan Valley

Roughly 700 years after Sodom is destroyed, the descendants of Abraham are led by Moses back from four centuries of exile in Egypt. The great comfort they first find in Egypt under the leadership of Joseph ultimately results in slavery.

Moses rescues them, brings them to the borders of the homeland, and then dies. Now they are trudging back to the land of their ancestors under the leadership of Aaron. They walk through Moab and cross the Jordan River east of Jericho just 20 or so miles north of ancient Sodom.

We are not told the moral state of Jericho at this time, just that they are "unbelievers" (Heb. 11:31) and they are the first city west of the Jordan that Israel must defeat to claim their promised land:

> So Jericho was destroyed completely, burned to the ground except for the precious metals and iron and bronze vessels that were put into the treasury of the Eternal's house. But Joshua spared the life

of Rahab the prostitute, all her family, and all she had because she was faithful to the spies he had sent, and she lived among the Israelites from that day on. (Josh. 6:24-25) We are told it is "By faith the prostitute Rahab welcomed the *Hebrew* spies *into her home* so that she did not perish with the unbelievers" (Heb. 11:31). James adds that "Even Rahab the prostitute was made right with God by hiding the spies and aiding in their escape" (James 2:25).

Rahab's experience presents an interesting picture of God's grace. She is not just saved out of prostitution by her faith and obedience to God, she becomes a national hero. She marries an Israeli prince and becomes an ancestor of King David—and of Jesus.

Rahab lived about 3,200 years ago. This glimpse into her survival from Jericho some 700 years after Sodom is destroyed tells a story of hope for anyone guilty of sexual sin.

So when the Canaanite woman comes wailing to Jesus and begs Him to free her daughter from a demon, notice the gracious way Matthew describes the situation: "Jesus—*whose ancestors included Ruth and Rahab*—spoke *with kindness and insight.* **Jesus:**

Woman, you have great faith. And your request is done. And her daughter was healed, right then and from then on" (Matt.15:28).

The way Jesus loves this woman and her daughter is the way we are to love our neighbors who are slaves to homosexuality. We are to speak to them with kindness and insight. We are to pray for them. And we are to cast out their demons as discussed earlier by praying against Belial.

Chapter 8
Lovers for the Tribe of Benjamin

Judges 19 tells the gruesome story of a traveling man and his mistress who stop for a night in the town of Gibeah in Benjamin territory. The custom is to set up your tent and sleep in the city square unless a local family invites you into their home.

An old man who is not from the tribe of Benjamin yet lives in Gibeah, sees these travelers, asks about their circumstances, and takes them in. Here's what happens:

Old Man: Peace be with you. I will take care of everything you need, but do not spend the night in the square.

The old man took them home and fed their donkeys. They washed *the dust of the road from* their feet, ate, and drank. While they were eating and drinking, the men of the city, an evil assembly, surrounded the house and began beating on the door. They called to the owner.

Men of the City: Bring out *your guest,* the man whom you have welcomed into your house. We want to have sexual relations with him!

Old Man *(pleading with them):* I beg you. Don't do this wicked thing to the traveler I have welcomed into my care. I have a virgin daughter, and this man has a mistress. I will bring them out to you to do what you want with them, but don't dishonor my guest with your wickedness.

The men would not listen. At last the Levite seized his mistress and pushed her outside. They raped her repeatedly and abused her all night long until the sun came up, when they left her alone. Then the woman crept to the doorway of the house where her master had spent the night. She collapsed and lay there as the sun rose in the sky. Her master, at last, woke and rose; and when he went to the door to prepare to go on his way, there was his mistress, lying near the doorway, her hands on the threshold.

Levite: Get up. It's time for us to go.

But she could not answer him. He put her body on the donkey and set out for home.

When he reached his house, he went in and found a knife. Then holding her firmly, he cut her body up into twelve pieces, cut her limb from limb, and these he sent throughout Israel. *And as the pieces were received,* anyone who saw this *horrible display* said, "Nothing like this *outrage* has ever happened in Israel since we came up from the land of Egypt. Think about it, weigh it carefully, and decide what to do." (Judg. 19:20-30)

The sexual predators in this story are the offspring of Abraham's great grandson Benjamin, the youngest of Jacob's twelve sons. They are family, and Benjamin is the beloved "baby of the family." How can the other children of Israel show love for such family members who care nothing for others, live only to gratify their own lusts, and devote their lives to sexual abuse?

This is a tough question, and everyone who receives a portion of the corpse of the dead woman already knows the story of Abraham, Sodom, Lot and Rahab. They are working with plenty of knowledge and experience of similar circumstances from their past. They sense the need to wipe out these evil men just as God destroyed the evil men of Sodom.

They assemble an army of 400,000 troops and then send this message to the tribe of Benjamin: "Turn over those perverted men from Gibeah so we can put them to death and cleanse this evil from Israel!" (Judg. 20:13).

In response, the men of Benjamin gather 26,000 fighting men including a special force of 700 left-handed warriors "who could sling a stone so accurately that they could hit any target, no matter how small" (Judg. 20:16).

A bloody and extended battle ensues. The tribe of Benjamin is annihilated except for 600 men who "fled to the rock of Rimmon, where they remained for four months. *In the meantime,* the warriors of Israel had *done their best to* destroy the people of Benjamin, killing them, destroying their livestock, and burning every city and town they encountered" (Judg. 20:47-48).

What should be done with those 600 stranded men? Killing them would terminate one of the 12 great families in Israel. The people of Israel now want to preserve this family line, yet they have already pledged at the Mizpah council not to give wives to the men of Benjamin. So they return to Bethel, *house of God,* and ask God what to do, and here is what happens the next morning:

> The people of Israel were moved with pity toward their kin, the tribe of Benjamin.
> **Israelites:** *Look,* one tribe of Israel has been cut off from the rest of us. How can the survivors of Benjamin get wives, since we have all sworn by the Eternal not to give them our daughters? Are there any of the tribes of Israel that did not come up before the Eternal at Mizpah? (Judg. 21:6-8).

Since nobody is there from Jabesh-Gilead, they send troops there and capture 400 virgins, bring them to the camp of Shiloh, and proclaim peace to the men of Benjamin. With only 400 wives for 600 men, a follow-up plan is also hatched:

> **Israelite Elders:** What can we do to find more wives for the remaining men *of Benjamin,* since all the other Benjaminite women were destroyed? Benjamin must have heirs and survive, so that not a single tribe may disappear out of Israel. But we cannot give them our daughters, for we

87

have sworn curses on anyone of us who gives wives to *the men of* Benjamin.

Israelites: Look, there is a yearly festival of the Eternal in Shiloh, north of Bethel, to the east of the road that links Bethel to Shechem and to the south of Lebonah.

They told the Benjaminites to go and hide in the vineyards.

Israelites: Watch, and when the young women of Shiloh come out to participate in the dances, dash out, grab yourself a wife, and take her back home to Benjamin. Then if their brothers or fathers come to complain to us, we can say, "Be generous. We weren't able to capture enough brides for the men of Benjamin, so we needed more women. But none of you suffers the curse, since you didn't give your daughters of your own free will!"

So that is what the men of Benjamin did: they kidnapped wives for themselves from the dancers *at the festival* and took them back home, where they rebuilt their towns and lived in them again. (Judg. 21:19-23)

Through human effort these people first try to carry out the *justice* of God. Then they try to carry out the *grace* of God. They do it imperfectly, but they are trying to do for their brother Benjamin what they would want done for themselves. They try to weed sin out of their brothers' lives and replace it with love.

These men of Benjamin are apparently not looking for wives. They are likely gay, and some of them may have been involved in the gang rape of a woman until she died. But they have been nudged in a redemptive direction. When we first see them, they would rather have died than go straight; now they would rather take a wife than die. They have changed their minds.

The modern science of neuroplasticity studies the incredible flexibility of the human brain. It proves that human behaviors can be relearned. We now understand from research the same thing ancient people knew from experience, that the human brain is infinitely capable of adapting.

To a large extent, you are what you think. Behavior follows thought. If you can imagine a thing, you can do it. We saw in earlier chapters how Satan uses this human brain flexibility to twist and deceive those who follow him. Many people these days are exercising their prerogative to change their minds. Becoming gay is possible by embracing homosexual ideas, pursuing them, and practicing that lifestyle.

The reverse is also possible as shown in this story. Following their desperate fight for survival, the men of Benjamin who were raised in and surrounded by a homosexual culture embrace what is an alternative lifestyle to them—they go straight by aiming their brains in the direction of traditional marriage.

Providing wives for these 600 destitute men is the most loving thing the other tribes of Israel can think to do for them. What was unthinkable for these men a few months ago becomes possible, and perhaps desirable.

An earlier Bible narrative reveals that Benjamin is the last to receive his father's blessing, and it comes in the form of an observation: "Benjamin is a ravenous wolf, devouring prey by morning and dividing spoil in the evening" (Gen. 49:27).

A selfish man with selfish ambitions and selfish children, there is not a lot to love in this spoiled brat. Yet the other families of Jacob show love to the family of Benjamin many generations later in that darkest hour.

Because of this decision to love their gay neighbor and relative, good things eventually happen. Saul from the family of Benjamin becomes the first king of Israel (1 Sam. 9). Later still in Persia, God uses Mordecai and Esther, from the family of Benjamin, to rescue His people from death (Esther 2:5-7). And the Apostle Paul who writes the definition of love explored in an earlier chapter also comes from Benjamin (Rom. 11:1).

When we choose to act in love on behalf of our gay neighbors, we cannot predict the outcome. Abraham acts in love toward his gay neighbors and God destroys them all anyway. Israel acts in love toward its gay neighbors and God provides wives for them. Who can say what God will do for your gay neighbor as a result of the love you will show?

Chapter 9
Jeremiah and His Wayward Ones

One way to love your gay neighbor is to warn about the judgment to come. But as Jeremiah finds out, such words are often not interpreted as loving.

Jeremiah is known as the "weeping" prophet. During a period of more than 40 years spanning the lives of five kings of Judah, he cries in deep sorrow over the fate he sees coming to Jerusalem. He lives in a declining civilization like ours: The nation of Israel has suffered moral, political, and economic collapse and is now under attack from its eastern neighbor Babylon.

For Jeremiah to tell the king in Jerusalem that he will be defeated by King Nebuchadnezzar and taken as a prisoner to Babylon is like me, Dan, declaring that the president of the United States will be defeated by Islamic jihadists and taken as a prisoner to—Babylon.

Because of his bold message, Jeremiah is not deeply loved. He is accused by some to be a traitor. But he deeply loves those he witnesses to as he begs them to repent of their evil practices, obey God, and do what is right.

The scene in which one of Jeremiah's major predictions comes true reads as follows:

This is how Jerusalem fell: *When the Egyptian threat in the south was over,* King Nebuchadnezzar of Babylon brought his army *back* to Jerusalem and resumed the siege. When King Zedekiah of Judah and his troops saw *the Babylonians break through the wall on the north side of the city,* they fled under the cloak of darkness. But the Chaldean army *discovered this and* chased after Zedekiah, capturing him on the plains of Jericho. They took him to King Nebuchadnezzar [and he] was forced to watch as his own sons and the nobles of Judah were slaughtered right in front of him. *This was the very last thing he saw, because* Nebuchadnezzar then blinded the eyes of Zedekiah. This *blinded and humiliated* king was then placed in bronze shackles and carried off to Babylon. Back in Jerusalem, the Chaldean troops burned down the king's palace and the commoners' houses and then tore down the walls *of the city*. (Jer. 39: 1, 4-8)

Even after Jeremiah's most gruesome prophesy comes true, people still will not believe him concerning their own future. Some of those not deported to Babylon flee to a self-imposed exile in Egypt. Jeremiah goes along but is obliged to give them this message:

This is what the Eternal, Commander of *heavenly* armies and God of Israel, has to say: "You saw what happened to Jerusalem and the towns of Judah *when the people disobeyed Me.* I brought disaster upon them because of their wickedness, and now the cities are in ruins and no one dares to live there. The people infuriated Me when they burned incense and worshiped other *so-called* gods....

Time after time I would send My servants, the prophets, saying, 'Oh, stop doing these disgusting things. *You know* I hate them!' Still they refused to listen and ignored *what I had to say*; they refused to abandon their wicked ways..... That is why they are a desolate wasteland today."

And now the Eternal God, Commander of *heavenly* armies and God of Israel, asks: *"Why are you doing this to yourselves again?* Why are you bringing further disaster upon yourselves and all your people? For there will be no man or woman, no infant or child who will survive this onslaught and return to Judah *from this place.* Why do you stir up My anger with your handmade *idols* and the incense you burn to the gods here in the land of Egypt where you are determined to live? You will destroy yourselves and become objects of scorn and cursing to the nations of the earth..... To this day, I've seen no evidence of sorrow or regret *for what has been done by My people.* They have shown no reverence for Me, nor have they obeyed My law....."

Therefore, the Eternal, Commander of *heavenly* armies and God of Israel, now declares: "Look! I have decided to destroy you and bring disaster on all of Judah..... I will punish those living in Egypt with war, famine, and disease, just as I punished *unfaithful* Jerusalem. None of those who

made it out of Judah alive and fled to Egypt
will survive. None of them will escape *what
is coming....* (Jer. 44:2-14 abridged)

A large crowd gathers and tells Jeremiah they will not
listen to him or obey God. They say, "We will burn
incense and pour out our drink offerings to the queen
of heaven just as we have always done" (Jer. 44:17).

Jeremiah replies to them, "*Take a good look at*
the disaster that has come upon you. It happened
because you burned incense *to other gods* and sinned
against the Eternal. *It happened* because you refused
to obey His voice or follow His law and His decrees,
because you ignored His warnings" (Jer. 44:23).

Up until now all of Jeremiah's predictions serve
as warnings: *If* you keep sinning, this is what will
happen. But now the people have crossed a line and
there is no going back. God's reply to them through
Jeremiah is this:

I swear by My great name that no man
or woman of Judah now living in Egypt will
ever again invoke My name or begin an oath
with the words 'As the Eternal Lord lives!'
because I will watch over their lives to bring
harm, not good. All the Judeans living in

Egypt will suffer from war and famine until all have died...."

Here is a sign for you so that *you will know* I am going to punish you in Egypt. This way you can be sure that My threats against you *are not idle*—they will come true. *And this will be your sign:* watch as I hand over Pharaoh Hophra, king of Egypt, to his enemies who want to kill him, just as I handed over Zedekiah, king of Judah, to his enemy, Nebuchadnezzar, king of Babylon. (Jer. 44:26-27, 29-30).

It seems ironic that one who loves his neighbors as deeply as Jeremiah does must speak so many words of judgment against them. But when you speak for God, you must be faithful to the Voice of God. And if you know the Word of God, you don't need to be a prophet to recognize the consequences of sinful behavior.

Unfortunately, we have religious leaders in our time chatting it up with talk show hosts and fitting Jeremiah's description of prophets and priests whose words "reek with deceit" on issues of sexual identity: "They offer superficial words. They say, 'Peace, peace,' *as if all is well.* But there is no peace. Do they feel any shame for their disgraceful deeds? Absolutely not. My very own have forgotten how to blush" (Jer. 6:14-15).

The consequence of their deception "is that they will fall among the fallen *and be defeated*; when the time comes, they will stumble beneath the weight of My punishment; *They will know soon enough what they have done*" (Jer. 6:15).

Do the many sins of these false teachers and their hearers in the time of Jeremiah include homosexual behavior? Some Bible scholars think the lessons from Abraham and Lot and the tribe of Benjamin are so deeply respected that gay sin is not an issue in Israel for more than a thousand years. Other scholars feel homosexual sin persists but is not talked about directly.

The Bible frequently uses deliberately vague language when identifying sins of a rebellious people. For example, Ezekiel writes in a prophecy comparing Jerusalem with a harlot, "This was the sin of your *warped* sister, Sodom: She and her daughters were arrogant, gluttonous, and lazy. She never gave help to the poor and needy. They were prideful, and they did abhorrent things right in front of Me, *shamelessly and without remorse!*" (Ezek. 16:49-50).

"Abhorrent" is a word that covers a wide range of sins Ezekiel would rather not mention by name. His reference to Sodom is the closest he will go in openly mentioning homosexual behavior.

Similarly, the people in Jeremiah's time are guilty of such things as worshipping pagan gods (today we call it "New Age"), killing their children as sacrifices to demonic gods (today we call it abortion), and various sexual sins lumped into the wider language of immorality and adultery (today we call it, "adult" behavior).

Regardless of the sin, the loving message of Jeremiah is consistent: Repent. Stop doing wicked things you know God hates. Love the Lord your God with all your heart, soul, mind, and strength. Love your neighbor as yourself. Honor God and He will honor you.

But sin takes a powerful grip on people. They have no strength to resist in the beginning, and even less strength to escape once they have fallen deeply into its clutches. You may be their only hope, just as were the patriarchs we have talked about.

Abraham's love for his gay neighbors took on frantic dimensions. First he personally, physically rescues them from their enemies in a time of war.

Then he pressures God right down to the last available moment in the hope of saving them.

Lot's love for his gay neighbors is demonstrated by the fact that he lives among them and would have shared their fate had not the Messengers of God compelled him to flee with his wife and daughters.

The land of Israel's love for its gay brothers, the tribe of Benjamin, is demonstrated by their efforts to destroy the evil. As a result, a few willing survivors repent. This is the first success story recorded in the Bible—the remaining men of Benjamin turn to the model of marriage prescribed by God, and they and their children live to bless the world.

Jeremiah's love for his wayward neighbors takes the form of many decades of pleading with them to repent. Even though they ignore all his efforts on their behalf, he goes into exile with them into Egypt. They trample on his bleeding heart to the very end— but he never gives up his struggle to save them.

You join this noble company when you commit to loving your gay neighbor. Such love requires the courage without which no one can enter the City of God. This book invites you to boldly love those who may have never experienced authentic love before.

May the grace of the Lord Jesus empower each faltering step.

Chapter 10
Seeing Love in the Confusion

A common misconception passed around by people who don't know the Bible is that God in the Old Testament is a God of Wrath; God in the New Testament is a God of Love.

Wrong. God is Love in both the Old and New Testaments, and one expression of that love is wrath—like the kind you have. Without hesitation you will instantly kill the snake that is about to poison your beloved child. That is unconditional love—for the child. You feel differently about the snake.

The anger of God displayed in the Bible is some of the strongest evidence of His love. To show His people why He is angry, God says to the prophet Hosea, "Go and marry a woman who is a prostitute and have children who come from this unfaithfulness. *This will represent how* the land *of Israel* has abandoned Me and become a prostitute *to other masters!*" (Hos. 1:2).

From God's point of view, the commandments He gives Moses are a marriage contract between God and His chosen people. They are to love God only. But because the people have broken this marriage agreement, God tells Hosea, "They'll be active like whores, but have no children because they've rebelled in guarding Me and My ways" (Hos. 4:10). Such actions have consequences: "Because they sow the wind, they'll reap the whirlwind" (Hos. 8:7).

God is love. His anger is one symptom of that love. To know Him, you must learn to distinguish between His unconditional *love* for you and your naïve assumption that He offers unconditional *acceptance* of your sin. In fact, your sin profoundly offends Him. Jesus loves the woman who commits adultery, but He doesn't unconditionally accept her sin.

Approving and legalizing evil is far different from tolerating evil. Paul loves the immoral man in 1 Corinthians 5—so much so that he doesn't unconditionally accept his sin. Instead, he hands him over to Satan. As my chaplain friend Ron Kopicko says, "Better to be worked over by Satan on this side of eternity if that is what it takes for him to repent, rather than an eternity of separation from the Lord."

The term "unconditional" is not a useful way to describe the love that comes from God. He pays the penalty for sin unconditionally—anyone who repents can come to Him. But repentance is the requirement—the condition—for taking advantage of that love.

To say that God has done everything necessary to overcome sin and pave the way to heaven for you is not the same as to say everyone will be saved. Jesus explains this very well in His story about the king who prepares a wedding feast for his son. Everyone is invited, but few came.

One guest at the wedding is disrespectful of wearing the purity symbolized by the wedding gown he is offered but fails to wear. The king whose son is getting married says about the imposter, "Tie him up, and throw him out into the outer darkness, where there is weeping and grinding of teeth." Jesus ends the story saying, "Many are invited, but few are chosen" (Matt. 22:13-14).

So forget about using the word "unconditional" when talking about the love of God. It only creates confusion. Satan loves confusion.

The culture you live in today is profoundly confused on the issue of sexuality. If you are confused and astonished at how quickly the homosexual agenda took over Europe and America, consider this story Jesus tells about the kingdom of heaven:

Once there was a farmer who sowed good seeds in his field. While the farmer's workers were sleeping, his enemy crept into the field and sowed weeds among all the wheat seeds. Then he snuck away again. Eventually the crops grew—wheat, but also weeds. So the farmer's workers said to him, "Sir, why didn't you sow good seeds in your field? Where did these weeds come from?"

"My enemy must have done this," replied the farmer.

"Should we go pull up all the weeds?" asked his workers.

"No," said the farmer. "*It's too risky*. As you pull up the weeds, you would probably pull up some wheat as well. We'll let them both grow until harvest time. I will tell the harvesters to collect the weeds and tie them in bundles to be burned, and only then to harvest the wheat and bring it to my barn." (Matt. 13:24-30)

Seeds of the sexual revolution planted in the 20th century are all reaching maturity at the same time. The experience of the weeds is that the field has always belonged to them—summer is the only season they know. Yet the farmer knows an autumn day for burning the weeds and bringing in the crop is as certain as the next harvest moon.

God seldom acts quickly; He acts suddenly. He gives absolutely no warning to all the gay neighbors in Sodom that they will be incinerated in a moment. He warns only the few people He will save. Why? Because things perfectly obvious to Abraham and Lot are inconceivable to the people of Sodom. In the same way, things perfectly obvious to you are inconceivable to your gay neighbors.

To Jeremiah, it must seem that God is very slow to act. God announces what He plans to do with incredible detail—then He delays the actual event with incredible patience. But when the time comes, King Zedekiah is bound and blinded and his family killed in one day.

To comprehend how badly things have gone, simply step back into God's all-knowing point of view. Compare the first Melchizedek, king of Jerusalem, with Zedekiah, a later king of Jerusalem.

One king is the very image of God; the other is the very image of Satan. In His love for humanity in general, God must ultimately destroy such corruption.

An example of God's sudden action appears in Ezekiel 9. Due to intense corruption, six men with deadly weapons and a man dressed in white linen and holding a writing kit enter the temple and stand at the altar. The glory of the Lord rises away from the winged guardian called cherub that guards the altar and moves to the doorway of the temple.

The Lord tells the writer to go through Jerusalem "and put a mark on the forehead of all those who are grieved by the shocking things going on in the city" (Ezek. 9:4). The writer does, and then the six heavenly executioners slaughter everyone who has not received the mark. "The executioners started by killing the elders in front of the sanctuary" (Ezek. 9:6).

Your gay neighbors may be unaware of their precarious situation in relation to God. They may even attend an organization labeled "church" that accepts their homosexual behavior. They may in fact worship under the leadership of gay clergy. Your gay neighbor might even *be* a gay pastor.

Such individuals explain away portions of the Bible that disturb or confront them. They make gods of themselves by standing in the place of God. Instead of receiving the Bible as guidance from God, they twist the verses to provide for themselves excuses from God. They would rather not learn obedience or allow the Word to flay their hearts.

Satan is very gifted at teaching such people to twist the Scriptures. He has long experience and great skill in deception. As he tempts Jesus in the wilderness, he demonstrates deep knowledge of the Bible—as well as utter inability to interpret it correctly (see Matt. 4:1-11).

Your gay neighbors may be equally gifted at finding what they are looking for in the Bible. They may even be able to preach elaborate and passionate sermons demonstrating their brilliance. In so doing, they must deftly ignore vast portions of Scripture.

The tides of the Bible carry a strong undertow insisting on sexual purity defined as sexual abstinence. One exception exists: Christian marriage between one man and one woman. Submit to that undertow and you will be baptized: you will drown to yourself and live for the Anointed One. To resist that current you must swim sidewise to it. Like a pod of dolphins, some gay groups imagine themselves to be followers of Jesus while they frolic contrary-wise in these waters.

Just as you took God's point of view to compare Melchizedek with Zedekiah, you can stand in the same place and compare the New Testament Church with the compromised organizations in your neighborhood still branded "church." What they do is blasphemy. Their leaders do not have the mark of God on their forehead—more likely they wear rainbow ties. Flee such places and persons, for when God executes justice He will begin with them.

The Church is the Body of Jesus the Anointed One and exists to tell the story of God and bring salvation, healing, and ultimately eternal life to all who obey. There is a big difference between being cleansed by the tides of Scripture rather than desperately swimming sidewise to the undertow.

You do not have the ability to untwist what your gay neighbors twist. Do not argue with them and the views they assemble as defenses on every side. Avoid all such confusion.

Again, prayer is your only way forward, just as it was for my friend Anne Paine Root who says, "Losing a son through AIDS changed the way I view God, the world, myself, my family, and the problem of sin. I am more aware than before of Satan's hatred of God. He is obsessed with destroying God's creatures and creation. My son Samuel lost his health, his eyesight, and his future to the enemy of his soul."

Her experience leads Anne to observe, "For every Christian counselor who was equipped to confront our son with the true nature of his problem there were hundreds of voices telling him to accept himself 'as you are.'"

Toxoplasmosis had already spread its lesions from Samuel's optic nerves to his brain, and his official diagnosis was downgraded from HIV to AIDS before this 24-year old Marine could muster the courage to call his mom and say, "Mother, I need to pray."

Anne reports, "Samuel asked God for forgiveness and turned the tattered remnants of his life over to the One who had so faithfully, patiently, and lovingly wooed him. Five months after he received the promise of redemption and only a few weeks after he had witnessed his choice through the rite of baptism, Samuel quietly took his last breath. We gathered as a family to return the remains of his disease-ravaged body to the ground and commit his redeemed soul to the God who gave him to us for a time."

Loving your gay neighbors with a mother's love is what it will take. Let the Lord mark your forehead with that sort of compassion. The heavy deception covering their eyes will not fall away by argument. It may fall away in answer to prayer through the authority of the Holy Spirit.

This is where Jesus enters the picture.

Chapter 11
The Views of Jesus

Nicodemus is a theologian and scholar who suspects Jesus might be the Anointed One who the Bible predicts will save the world. Jesus confirms this hunch when he says to Nicodemus about Himself, "For God expressed His love for the world in this way: He gave His only Son so that whoever believes in Him will not face everlasting destruction, but will have everlasting life" (John 3:16).

If Jesus is God's full expression of love, and if you are going to love your gay neighbor, then a time must come when you will tell this neighbor about Jesus. When that time comes, there may be great confusion, because people these days do not understand tough love. They think "love" is a synonym for "tolerance."

They don't understand love because they haven't listened carefully to Jesus, the embodiment of love. They haven't heard Him say, "God didn't send His Son into the world to judge it; instead, He is here to rescue a world *headed toward certain destruction*" (John 3:17).

Our examples from the Old Testament were not judgmental regarding their gay neighbors. Likewise, Jesus has said He did not come to judge. And it is not our job to judge. Just like Abraham, and just like Jesus, it is the rescuing business we are in.

And yet, on many occasions, when we deliver the message of John 3:17, we will be accused of being judgmental. Perhaps we can clear up that misunderstanding by pointing out that we are not the judge—we are merely aware that judgment has already been passed.

The gavel has already fallen. The Bible speaks steadily of a verdict already handed down by the Judge of all people. That is why Jesus tells Nicodemus: "I'm not here to judge you—you've already been judged and are headed toward certain destruction. I'm here to rescue you!"

Rescue you from what? In this verse the rescue is from "certain destruction." In other verses it is from "the lake of fire" (Rev. 20:15). In the next verse we see the rescue is from "condemnation." Of all the individuals in the Bible, Jesus is the one who talks most about hell. He knows it as a vivid reality.

Jesus next says about Himself to Nicodemus, "Condemnation is already the reality for everyone who refuses to believe because they reject the name of the only Son of God" (John 3:18).

At this point your gay friends will say, "How can a loving God condemn anyone to hell? I refuse to believe in such a tyrant."

These individuals do not comprehend the magnitude of the problem of sin. Hell is the necessary restraint a loving God must place on those who hate Him to protect those who love Him. The tyrant is not the loving One who created hell but the hateful one who makes it necessary.

Whenever you must discuss this issue with an unbeliever, you will find yourself up against Satan's twisted thinking explored earlier. The world is full of deception, double-speak, and lies aimed at confusing people at the most basic level. The term "gay" provides a good example. It used to mean happy, carefree, and colorful. Now it describes a person who exchanges God's beautiful design for sex into its damaging opposite.

You are unlikely to help such a person by argument. A more effective approach is to simply continue explaining the definition of love that Jesus embodies. In fact, Jesus answers the gay person's question in His next phrase:

Why does God allow for judgment *and condemnation*? Because the Light, *sent from God*, pierced through the world's darkness *to expose ill motives, hatred, gossip, greed, violence, and the like*. Still some people preferred the darkness over the light because their actions were dark. Some of humankind hated the light. They *scampered hurriedly* back into the darkness where vices thrive and wickedness flourishes. Those who *abandon deceit and* embrace what is true, they will enter into the light where it will be clear that all their deeds come from God. (John 3:19-21).

Jesus is the greatest expression of God's love because He is sent to provide a way to escape from death, the penalty for sin. People who reject His light condemn themselves. There is some hope that merely by sharing this light with your gay neighbors, they will receive it, turn away from their devotion to fulfilling their own passions, and focus their new lives on walking in the light that Jesus provides.

Given the fact of damnation, Jesus is indeed the very embodiment of love.

Nicodemus now understands that Jesus is unique. His love is unique. His knowledge of hell is unique—and first hand. And His answer to the trick questions of some other religious leaders is unique. These rascals who do not believe in Him try to trip Him up with a question about divorce. They ask, "Is it ever lawful for a man to divorce his wife?" (Matt. 19:3). In reply Jesus not only answers the question about divorce, He also defines marriage:

> Haven't you read that in the beginning God created humanity male and female? *Don't you remember what the story of our creation tells us about marriage?* "For this reason, a man will leave his mother and father and cleave to his wife, and the two shall become one flesh." If a husband and wife are one flesh, *how can they divorce? Divorce would be a bloody amputation, would it not?* "What God has brought together, let no man separate." (Matt. 19:4-6)

The religious scholars press on, saying, "Why did Moses explain that if a man leaves his wife, then he must give her a certificate of divorce and send her away, free and clear of him?" (Matt. 19:7).

Jesus answers, "Moses permitted you to divorce your wives because your hearts were hard. *But divorce was an innovation, an accommodation to a fallen world.* There was no divorce at creation. Listen, friends: if you leave your wife, unless there is adultery, and then marry another woman, you yourself are committing adultery. *Only if there is adultery can you divorce your wife*" (Matt. 19:8-9).

Here Jesus trusts their logic to deduce that adultery is the thing that breaks the bond of marriage, and in such cases a legal divorce merely recognizes a separation that has already occurred.

So the religious scholars have their answer, and the disciples also draw their own conclusions, saying, "If this is how it is, then it is better to avoid marrying in the first place" (Matt. 19:10). They are recognizing marriage as an intensely serious, lifelong commitment requiring an enormous investment of time and energy.

That is my experience as well. Sometimes I am astonished at the amount of energy and commitment required to achieve success in marriage. I have come to this conclusion: Men are on the cutting edge of spiritual warfare whenever they actively work to improve their marriages by sacrificially loving their wives.

But Jesus is an unmarried, celibate man. He takes the discussion in the opposite direction by saying, "Not everyone can hear this teaching, only those to whom it has been given. *Some people do not marry, of course.* Some people are eunuchs because they are born that way, others have been made eunuchs by men, and others have renounced marriage for the sake of the kingdom of heaven. Anyone who can embrace that call should do so" (Matt. 19:11-12).

The term Jesus uses, *eunuchs*, technically means "castrated." Jesus says some people are born with limited sexual capacity, and it is fine for them not to marry.

Those "made eunuchs by men" may refer to physical injuries as well as to the common practice in that time of castrating slaves to protect their owners' women or to destroy the slave's ability to produce children.

And in the church there is a long tradition of those who choose celibacy in order to devote all the time and energy that a quality marriage would require into advancing the kingdom of heaven on earth.

When Jesus says, "Anyone who can embrace that *call* should do so," He affirms that celibacy—commitment to sexual inactivity—is a high calling from God. It is the way forward for any follower of Jesus who does not marry a person of the opposite gender. Jesus explains how it is possible to go through life observing the commandment not to commit adultery, and in His personal life He modeled that celibate lifestyle. Celibacy was the way of Jesus, the only perfect man.

This biblical expectation of celibacy does not play well in a heavily sexualized world. While homosexual marriage is legal in some countries, this is not different from the thoroughly pagan governments in which the New Testament Church found itself.

That Jesus says nothing more about homosexuality may be a reflection of the absence of such behavior in Israel at that time. He only responds to actual circumstances He personally faces during His short lifetime. Some New Testament writers address homosexuality directly because they encounter it during the missionary movement into the pagan Greek and Roman worlds.

The Holy Spirit writes to the church in Thyatira by the hand of John, "I have this against you: you have tolerated that woman Jezebel, who is a self-anointed prophetess and who misleads My followers to commit immoral sexual acts" (Rev. 2:20). This term "Jezebel" calls to mind the wife of King Ahab who murdered the prophets of God and worshipped Baal and other sexually immoral gods. She is an expert on "the deep things of Satan" (Rev. 2:24).

One day at the climax of a war, Jezebel is sitting in her window and a warrior of God shouts up to her, "Is anyone *in this city* on my side?" A few eunuchs who serve the queen throw her out the window where Jehu tramples her with his horse and her body is eaten by dogs (See 2 Kings 9:31-33).

Similarly, the Holy Spirit says regarding the Jezebel in Thyatira, "I have provided her enough time to turn away *from her indecency*, but she refuses to turn from these immoral acts" (Rev. 2:21). Great affliction is promised to her and death to her children so that "Through this all the churches will know I am the One who *relentlessly* explores the mind and heart, and I will deal with each of you as you deserve according to your acts" (Rev. 2:23).

We should participate with God in loving our gay neighbors with the understanding that God is providing them this time in which to repent, just as He did for Jezebel. But we should not let those we truly love imagine that the current period of grace is a permanent state. A day is coming when those who practice homosexual behaviors will suffer horrific punishment.

Understand this: The sexually charged world you live in today is not new. The fertility cults have ancient roots. Sex as a religion is a deeply ingrained practice everywhere the good news of Jesus has not penetrated. And people obsessed with sexual identity will establish sex as a religion in those places where the good news once prospered but is now abandoned.

Your gay neighbors are caught up in this loss of identity. Without the love that you can show them by explaining the new world realities introduced in the Bible, they may never find their way to wholeness. And talking to them about this will be difficult. However, not talking about it is almost impossible as soon as you open your Bible.

Large sections of New Testament books such as Romans, Ephesians, Colossians, James, and Jude are devoted to instructions regarding sexual and moral purity in personal life. Paul goes so far as to say, "*Listen,* don't let any kind of immorality be breathed among you" (Eph. 5:3).

Breathe prayers instead. Before His death, Jesus prayed a wonderful prayer for His followers. One thing He said to His Father about us is this: "Like Me, they are not products of the corrupt world order. Immerse them in the truth, the truth Your voice speaks. In the same way You sent Me into this world, I am sending them" (John 17:16-18).

You are sent to love all your neighbors, including your gay ones. If you ever wonder whether your actions truly demonstrate love, ask yourself this question: Do I always act in their best interest? This test of love pinpoints motives. Some people presume they are acting in love when in fact they are being selfish—wanting something rather than offering something. Or they are being proud—wanting to acquire status or respect. Or they are being thoughtless—not caring sufficiently for that person.

However, "A *true* friend loves regardless of the situation, and a *real* brother exists to share the tough times" (Prov. 17:17). Showing such love involves a level of faithfulness not shown in casual relationships. As the writer of Proverbs 27:6 says, "Wounds inflicted by *the correction of* a friend prove he is faithful; the abundant kisses of an enemy show his lies."

With so many ways to fail in truly loving, it would be easy at this point to give up the battle. With so many ways of being misunderstood, the safe path is to simply ignore your gay neighbors and hope they ignore you.

With so many ways to fail, you might as well just give up. Your gay neighbors will very likely call you derogatory names and write you off as a lunatic or fanatic—just as they did with Jeremiah—and just as they did with Jesus. You cannot love your gay neighbors at this level on your own strength. You are bound to fail.

Only the Holy Spirit can help you now. Invite Him into the situation. Ask Him to take over the relationship between you and your neighbor. Know that loving requires great wisdom, perception, and listening. Before speaking, ask yourself, is what I have to say kind? Is it thoughtful? Is it necessary? Is the timing right?

To love is to say the right thing, at the right time, in the right way, for the right reasons. Jesus somehow managed to do this all the time. I manage to do it once in a while.

Learning to love your gay neighbor will take a lifetime of growing each day more and more into the image of Jesus by the power of the Holy Spirit. And it may help if you can get a bigger picture of what that love will involve.

Book III: The Gay Picture

Chapter 12
Loving After the *Ball*

Loving as the world loves is merely to exchange favors. Loving as God loves is spiritual warfare.

You may not be loved back. What will you do then? Will you turn to the world's pornographic how-to books on loving? Pages from them will drift in the wind past the cross where you are being crucified.

If you are to step into this crucible, you must come prepared. You must know this enemy of your soul who you must love. In this climax to a book on loving, I will show you the techniques the gay world has used to resist God's love so that when those strategies are used against you, you will know how to respond.

These methods are outlined in the book, *After the Ball: How America Will Conquer Its Fear and Hatred of Gays,* by Marshall Kirk and Hunter Madsen (Doubleday, NY: 1989). The authors are Harvard graduates who specialize in public persuasion tactics and social marketing.

Ball describes itself as the "gay manifesto" that will transform America. You must understand the worldview of *Ball* or your efforts to love your gay neighbors will fail. *Ball* assumes that all "natural" human behaviors are wholesome and right and good and ought to be accepted and encouraged. It brands as "bigot" anyone who doesn't agree.

For example, to brand a message from evangelist Franklin Graham "hate speech" is merely to follow the instructions featured in the *After the Ball* playbook. Expect them to call this book you are reading now "hate speech" and its author a "bigot." Of course, it should be clear to you who is using the actual hate speech. And it does not come as a surprise. Jesus said to His audience on the way to His crucifixion, "For if they treat Me like this when I'm like green unseasoned wood, what will they do to a nation that's ready to burn like seasoned firewood?" (Luke 23:31).

What will you do when the name-calling begins in response to the love you show? This is only the beginning of the verbal abuse you may experience. We are just in the introduction of *Ball* and it is already calling you a bigot, and now it will invent its own term to further label you. Here are words from page xxiv: "'Homophobia' is a comforting word, isn't it? It suggests that our enemies...are actually scared of us.... The very term 'phobia' ridicules our enemies (and intentionally so)."

Ball adds this clarification: "We've cast about in vain for a term that would, at once, (a) clearly signify 'homo-hatred' for the layman, (b) satisfy the pedant's demand for etymological consistency, and (c) for everyone, look as impressively scientific and clinical as the term 'homophobia'" (xxv).

Some facts: A "phobia" is an irrational fear—and "propaganda" consists of deliberate lies repeated often enough that they are assumed true. *Ball* has swayed a nation to believe a lie. You are not irrationally fearful of your gay neighbor. You love your gay neighbor, but a campaign of war is arrayed against you. *Ball* says, "The campaign we outline in this book, though complex, depends centrally upon a program of unabashed propaganda, firmly grounded in long-established principles of psychology and advertising" (xxviii).

Too much time in the world and too little time in the Word will turn your heart of love into feet of clay. Realize you are not the first to face such opposition:

There is nothing sacred, and no one is safe.
Vicious sarcasm drips from their lips; they
bully and threaten to crush their enemies.
They even mock God as if He were not
above; their arrogant tongues boast
throughout the earth; they feel invincible.
Even God's people turn and are carried
away by them; they watch and listen, yet
find no fault in them. (Ps. 73:8-10)

Ball confronts you with an assumption about
morality that "when it comes to fighting the charge
that *homosexuality is statistically abnormal hence
immoral*, there is strength in numbers" (17) and
argues that perhaps ten percent of the population is
gay. *Ball* shows no awareness that a thing may be
intrinsically wrong regardless of public opinion or
majority approval.

Remember that in Genesis 18, God informs
Abraham He intends to destroy Sodom. He tells
Abraham, "For the sake of only 10, I still will not
destroy it," yet He *does* destroy the city. Notice the
compassion of both Abraham and Lot toward the
majority population despite blatant homosexual
aggression against them, even to the point where the

men of Sodom attempt to rape the messengers of God (Gen. 19:5).

Your gay neighbors are fully armed with excuses provided by *Ball*, which asserts that "sexual orientation usually is set at an early age and cannot be changed," linking it to racial identity with the remark that "to become a Negro is a weighty act" (32). The claim that behavior is as genetic as race is repeated so often that the general public assumes it is true. But as yet scientific research has yet to turn up a "gay" gene.

A belief *Ball* instills in your mind is that "Sexual feelings are not really chosen by anybody: homosexuality is just as healthy and natural for some persons as heterosexuality is for others" (107).

Driven by sexual passion, *Ball* cannot comprehend a life of obedience to Divine calling, or submission to a higher order than natural instincts. However, the things you know from the Bible are not ideas that can fluctuate based on persuasion, propaganda, intimidation, name calling, or any other bullying technique.

Ball is not up against simply what you think or *feel* or *imagine* as true or *wish* were true. Eternal facts and timeless truths from God can't be shaken by political pull, social machinery, or propaganda campaign.

Only your consistent life and unfailing love will open such truths to your gay neighbor. Without your witness, they cannot comprehend that God offers redemption and restoration to all who confess and forsake their sin, seeking His mercy and forgiveness through Jesus Christ.

The reason to believe things explained in the Bible is not because they feel good or are easy, traditional, or safe. Believe them because they stand at the core of 6,000 years of salvation history and are unlikely to waiver in the face of the homosexual political propaganda.

In many circumstances, the gay world functions on reverse morality and reverse logic. Their objective is to turn the world upside down in a way that may actually make you feel guilty about being heterosexual. They tell you it is worse for you to judge evil than for them to do evil. They pretend to inhabit the moral high ground.

The next thing you may be accused of is prejudice. Since prejudice is a learned behavior, you will be informed that your objections to homosexuality are nothing more than learned behavior. Since you learned it, you can un-learn it. Therefore, one agenda of the gay world is to gain acceptance through behavior modification—not of their own behavior, but of yours!

Of course, followers of Jesus are on a path of continual behavior modification as they work daily to adjust their lives to become more like their Savior. This is different from the "jamming" propaganda technique used in the gay world to change the behaviors of other people. *Ball* states that it wants to create internal conflict in the minds of "bigots" to achieve an "incompatible emotional response" so that "normal people feel *shame* when they are not thinking, feeling, or acting like one of the pack" (151).

Shame on you for being intolerant of the growing social acceptance of homosexuality! *Ball* transcends morality for itself but wants you (and God) to feel naughty for that despicably judgmental attitude of yours: "The trick is to get the bigot into the position of feeling a conflicting twinge of shame" (151).

You may be told that you are using "hate speech" when you say things that guide a gay person toward conversion to biblical faith. Yet they are using the same language and strategies to convert you. They write:

> By Conversion we actually mean something far more profoundly threatening to the American Way of Life, without which no truly sweeping social change can occur. We mean conversion of the average American's emotions, mind, and will, through a planned psychological attack, in the form of propaganda fed to the nation via the media. (153)

You may not realize that your conversion is the stated objective of the gay world, but listen to *Ball*:

> In Conversion, the bigot, who holds a very negative stereotypic picture, is repeatedly exposed to literal picture/label pairs, in magazines, and on billboards and TV, of gays—explicitly labeled as such!—who not only don't look like his picture of a homosexual, but are carefully selected to look either like the bigot and his friends, or like any one of his other stereotypes of all-right guys. (154)

Everyone who is not with them is said to suffer from homophobia and homohate—animals needing psychological reconditioning. They react violently to the idea that psychological reconditioning is either possible or desirable for a homosexual, yet they devote an entire chapter to proposing how such psychological reconditioning can and must be carried out against the entire heterosexual population.

The propaganda strategy outlined "relies more upon emotional manipulation than upon logic" (162), Outright lies are discussed next, with warnings to be careful with these, because they are easily found out, on the one hand, yet "certain lies become hallowed public myths, persisting for as long as the public chooses to believe them" (163).

I am not misrepresenting this book. I am merely summarizing major points. Here is a full paragraph to reveal the underbelly of the gay movement:

When, in a 1985 *Christopher Street* article, we presented a blueprint for a national propaganda effort, doubters derided the proposal as irrelevant or impotent, the methods as demeaning and fraudulent, and our intent as reactionary. In February 1988, however, a "war conference" of 175 leading gay activists, representing organizations from across the land, convened in

Warrenton, Virginia, to establish a four-point agenda for the gay movement. The conference gave first priority to "a nation-wide media campaign to promote a positive image of gays and lesbians" (*Ball* 163).

If you feel like you have a target drawn large on the back of your head—no wonder! Someone has declared war on you, whether you believe it or not. Your task in response is to love your enemies, even when pro-gay advertising shows a picture of someone in a white KKK robe and the text, "Some guys have trouble accepting gay people" (245).

The love you express to your gay neighbor will not always be well received, just as the love God expresses to the world He created is often rejected. In a section called "The Rejection of Morality," *Ball* quotes Oscar Wilde who said, "The only way to get rid of temptation is to yield to it" (289).

Ball only recognizes two alternatives for the person with a same sex attraction. "He can (1) accept the received values of conventional morality and hate himself, or (2) step outside the conventional way of looking at things, begin to think for himself and form his own values, realize that the Judeo-Christian prejudice against homosexuality is arbitrary, absurd, and evil, and, by rejecting it, replace his self-hatred with self-esteem" (290). *Ball* writes that "many—we hope most—gays eventually reach this stage of maturity" (290).

Notice the "either-or" logical fallacy in the above paragraph. The two options identified are not your only choices. You can accept conventional morality and *not* hate yourself by instead repenting of the hateful thing about yourself and sacrificing it on the altar of obedience to the God who made you and loves you. This act places you in the company of all those who in response to the grace of God see their shame replaced by honor, their guilt replaced by innocence, their fear overcome by the power of God.

The Lord says to false prophets through Ezekiel, "I will save My people from your *seductive* powers" (Ezek. 13:23). He will do this because the false prophets "have encouraged the wicked instead of showing them the error of their ways so they could live" (Ezek. 13:22).

You can refute the seductive powers of deception from the likes of Oscar Wilde. What he said is not true: yielding to temptation is not the only way to get rid of it. Such yielding only leads to more and more temptation. The way to get rid of temptation is to turn it over to your Lord Jesus. Ask Him to fill you with the power of His Holy Spirit. Ask Him to help you "Stay focused on what's above, not on earthly things" (Col. 3:2). Set your mind where the Anointed One stands at the right hand of God, always praying for you.

The paragraph from *Ball* quoted above highlights the intense level of spiritual warfare within the gay world. The quote reflects the demonic blathering of those cast out of heaven and spewing Divinity-phobia. Pride indeed went before Lucifer, the Angel of Light who was tossed out of heaven, and here it is explicitly stated by gays that homosexual behavior is the demonic substitute of God's created order. The origins of "Gay Pride" are very clear.

Ball next acknowledges that "the gay community has no generation-to-generation continuity" (364) and attributes this "wretched situation" to "the complete absence, in the gay lifestyle, of anything corresponding to family" (365).

The family model put forward by *Ball* suggests that a male of age 30 or so (*erastes*—the adult lover) become the mentor and adult role model of a youth of 17 or so (*eromenos*—the beloved) in "an alliance partaking equally of the qualities of father-son, teacher-student, and big brother-little brother relationships... with the superadded bond of explicitly sexual love" (367).

Ball desires that in the normal course of events the young man would marry, sire children, and in his adulthood perhaps establish "a fresh alliance, in turn, with a younger male" (368). This is the envisioned future of gay marriage—a state-recognized system for a self-perpetuating institution of homosexuality.

Ball's vision of love is far different from the one you find in the Bible. It is defiled, sacrilegious, and deceptive, and it is not the kind of love you will find walking the streets of the City of God. One aspect of that City is described as follows: "Nothing that defiles or is defiled can enter into its *glorious gates*. Those who practice sacrilege or deception will never walk its streets" (Rev. 21:27).

The love you have to show your gay neighbor is bound to be misunderstood, judged, and rejected. In this circumstance your best move is to do what Abraham did—and what Lot, Jeremiah, and Jesus did—love them anyway.

Chapter 13
Paul Loves His Gay Neighbors

The homosexual model for family put forward by *Ball* in the previous chapter comes from practices in some ancient Greek and Roman civilizations. The Church has already encountered this circumstance and knows how to love these gay neighbors.

The Apostle Paul writes to the Romans that a time comes when God gives up on certain people:

So God gave them just what their lustful hearts desired. *As a result,* they violated their bodies and invited shame into their lives. *How?* By choosing a foolish lie over God's truth. They gave their lives and devotion to the creature rather than to the Creator Himself, who is blessed forever and ever. Amen. This is why God released them to their own vile pursuits, *and this is what happened*: they chose sexual counterfeits— women had sexual relations with other women and men committed unnatural, shameful acts because they burned with lust for other men. This sin was rife, and they suffered painful consequences. (Rom. 1:24-27)

This is a frightening text, for it shows that a time comes when God says "enough!" He said "enough" about the world in the time of Noah, and Paul writes that God says "enough" about some people in his time:

> Since they had no mind to recognize God, He turned them loose to follow the unseemly designs of their depraved minds and to do things that should not be done. Their days are filled with all sorts of godless living, wicked schemes, greed, hatred, endless desire for more, murder, violence, deceit, and spitefulness. And, *as if that were not enough,* they are gossiping, slanderous, God-hating, rude, egotistical, smug people who are always coming up with even more dreadful ways to treat one another. They don't listen to their parents; they lack understanding *and character.* They are simple-minded, covenant-breaking, heartless, and unmerciful; *they are not to be trusted.* Despite the fact that they are fully

aware that God's law says this way of life
deserves death, they fail to stop. And
worse—they applaud others on this
destructive path. (Rom. 1:28-32)

Paul could be describing cable or network television,
but he is writing to the Romans two thousand years
ago. No doubt some of them branded his description
of their lives as "hate speech."

How does Paul love his gay neighbors with such
language? He loves them by seeing what is really
going on and warning them of the consequences of
their behavior. He writes, "the wrath of God is
breaking through from heaven, opposing all
manifestations of ungodliness and wickedness by the
people who do wrong to keep God's truth in check"
(Rom. 1:18).

They are not just doing wrong to gratify their
desires—they are purposefully opposing God's truth.
They are unashamed, so Paul is equally unashamed.
He knows what he says is controversial yet
necessary. He writes, "For I am not *the least bit*
embarrassed about the gospel. *I won't shy away from
it*, because it is God's power to save every person who
believes" (Rom. 1:16).

Paul knows that the best way to help troubled people is to share good news with them, and he knows why such sharing is helpful. "You see," he says, "in the good news, God's restorative justice is revealed. *And as we will see,* it begins with and ends in faith. As the Scripture declares, 'By faith the just will obtain life'" (Rom. 1:17).

Paul loves his gay neighbors in Rome with great passion and persistence. He goes there and spends the final years of his life sharing the Good News he knows with these terribly confused and deceived people.

And how do they thank him? Of course, many believe and a great church is established. But for Paul personally, it does not go so well. In the end the Roman government executes him.

Jesus said in John 15:13, "There is no greater way to love than to give your life for your friends."

This book is not about what becomes of you as a result of loving your gay neighbor. It's about what becomes of your neighbor. Ultimately, everybody dies. Think about that and plan accordingly.

Meanwhile, in many situations my expectation is that both you and your gay neighbor will be transformed. I would like to end this book on a realistic note about that.

Chapter 14
The Hair Dresser Report

You met Brenda and Denny in the introduction. As this book goes to press, Denny is in rehab for a stroke he experienced at work. For some time he lost all feeling in his left side and could barely talk. He is regaining some mobility in his arm and hand, though he still cannot move his leg or stand. His speech is returning, but it's difficult.

In fact, everything is difficult. Denny reports that his sexual orientation has not changed. It is a cross he carries in the same way that unmarried heterosexuals must carry the burden of their sexual temptations.

Denny's close friends for many years have been gay, and they are still his friends. They are good and kind people. He has experienced care and community from some of them. Denny has no romantic involvement and lives celibate.

Going through this experience with him, his pastor, Brenda, has come to see that many Christians have a very warped attitude toward homosexuals.

Brenda says the militant, perverted, loud mouths poorly represent most of them, who just want to be valued and not treated badly. To lump them all into one category is like them lumping all followers of Jesus into a fanatically judgmental category. Many homosexuals are people who are a blessing to know and easy to love. The sins of heterosexuals are different than those of homosexuals, but we are all sinners in need of the same Savior.

Before Denny's stroke, a wonderful thing happened. Brenda's adult daughter, Rachel, and Danny have become very good friends (he does her hair, too). Rachel's three-year-old son goes with her and gets his haircut as well. Little Max loves Denny. Denny always gives him candy. Max reminds his parents every night to pray for Denny.

One day Denny confides to Rachel of his longing for someone to be a special friend—a confidant—someone to grow with and occasionally have dinner with. There would be no romantic expectations or desires.

Rachel commits to pray with him about that, and to believe that God will bring him a special female friend. Just before his stroke, Pastor Brenda has an appointment with a lovely lady about his age in the church. Marge is divorced, a committed follower of Jesus, and a regular and capable volunteer. She has no interest in remarriage. However, in the appointment she shares of her desire for occasional male companionship. She explains that true friendships with both genders are most satisfying. She expresses her disappointment that she doesn't know a male Christian willing to be just a friend.

Immediately Denny comes to mind. Brenda tells her of his full circumstance, and without blinking an eye Marge says, "I will pray for God to open the right opportunity."

But within two weeks, Denny has the stroke. None of the expected opportunities open. But Marge feels led to go visit him, even though they have never met. They develop a fast friendship. Strangely enough, she had once been very depressed and was placed in the same rehab center.

Marge has great empathy for Denny. She visits regularly, takes him his favorite fish sandwiches, has dinner with him, and helps him do therapy. She says it's just what the doctor ordered for her. And Denny has thanked Brenda and God many times for sending Marge to him.

Brenda concludes, "I love gays—but not nearly as much as Jesus does. I can always count on Him to do miracles."

Brenda adds, "I am infuriated at the repeated sexual sin among leaders and Christians who have legitimate, God-blessed ways to satisfy their desires. The shame of the Church in our generation is our own obsession with sex while we castigate the same obsession among homosexuals."

Obsession with sex—we are right back there with the Corinthians. And it is the Apostle Paul who identifies exactly how to love all your neighbors. In addition to his gracious, loving words quoted earlier, he writes the following to the same audience—a fitting conclusion to this book about why it is so vital to love your gay neighbor:

> Do you need reminding that the unjust have no share in the blessings of the kingdom of God? Do not be misled. A lot of people stand to inherit nothing of God's coming kingdom, including those whose lives are defined by sexual immorality, idolatry, adultery, sexual deviancy, theft, greed, drunkenness, slander, and swindling. Some of you used to live in these ways, but

you are different now; you have been
washed clean, set apart, restored, *and set on*
the right path in the name of the Lord Jesus,
the Anointed, by the Spirit of our living God.
(I Cor. 6:9-11)

You are different now. You see how to love as God loves. You understand the problem of sin the way God understands it. As God explains to Ezekiel:

"'As I live,' says the Eternal Lord, 'I don't enjoy watching the wicked die; I want the wicked to stop doing what they're doing and live! Repent! Turn from your wicked ways. Why would you choose to die?'" (Ezek. 33:11).

You are different now. Perhaps, as you live out the love of God in this fallen world, your gay neighbor—like Brenda's friend Denny—will respond to that love and be different as well.

Context

It is good to wait quietly for the Eternal to make things right *again*.

It is good to have to deal with restraint and burdens when young.

Just leave in peace the one who waits in silence, *patiently* bearing the burden of God;

Just don't interfere if he falls, gape-mouthed in the dust. There may well be hope yet.

Just let him offer his cheek when struck. Let him be the butt of jokes.

—Lamentations 3:26-30

About the Author

Daniel V. Runyon is monk-like, spending mornings in his scriptorium, afternoons in his garden, evenings in fellowship, and nights sleeping with his wife. All of it is worship.

He has an M.A. from Wheaton College, Illinois, and a Ph.D. from Keele University, England. He is an authority on the writings of the Puritan writer John Bunyan and author of many specialized books, essays, and magazine articles.

The story of God summarized here is explored more deeply in his novel *The Shattered Urn: An Allegorical History of the Universe.* A full review of the book *After the Ball* appears in his book *Gay Marriage Considerations.* These and some of his other works are available online. Search Amazon.com: Daniel V. Runyon: Books.

Made in the USA
Lexington, KY
29 July 2018